The French Revolution

The French Revolution

R . BEN JONES

FUNK & WAGNALLS, NEW YORK

The French Revolution

PREFACE

This is a short book on a very complex subject. It follows in outline the main story of the Revolution, but analyses the different factors bearing upon the major crises. There is a bewildering variety of interpretations of the Revolution, and little attempt is made in this book to tabulate them; but at the end of each Section appears a short bibliography of the more important works that should be consulted for more detailed study. A useful brief introduction to changing fashions in interpretation is the Historical Association pamphlet, *Interpretations of the French Revolution* by George Rudé (1961). A synthesis of much recently published original work is given in the present volume, but the interpretation is coloured by the author's own views.

General histories of the Revolution abound. Louis Madelin's work, although old-fashioned, is good for a 'conservative' interpretation. Albert Mathiez (English translation, Phillips, New York, 1928) demonstrates a deeper view, inspired by Marxist ideas. Georges Lefebvre has written the best synthesis, although it presupposes prior knowledge: it is published in English in two volumes, *The French Revolution, From its Origins to 1793* (Routledge, 1962) and *From 1793 to 1799* (Routledge, 1964). J. M. Thompson's volume (Blackwell, 1951), contains a great deal of information; a shorter volume by Professor A. Goodwin (Hutchinson, 1958) concentrates on the early part of the Revolution at the expense of the war years. The relevant sections in the *New Cambridge Modern History*, Vols. VIII and IX (both 1965) should be read.

Lack of space precludes extensive quotation in this book from contemporary documents. A wide variety has been published. Most libraries will have H. Morse-Stephens's *Speeches of the Statesmen and Orators of the Revolution, 1789 to 1795* (2 Vols., Oxford University Press, 1892), and J. M. Thompson's *French Revolutionary Documents, 1789 to 1794* (Blackwell, 1933, reissued 1948); a fuller, well edited series is J. H. Stewart's *Documentary Survey of the French Revolution* (Collins-Macmillan, 1951). Many volumes of letters and memoirs, not always reliable, exist; among the more important are Arthur Young's *Travels in France* (ed. Maxwell, Cambridge University Press, 1929); *Correspondance entre le Comte de Mirabeau et le Comte de la Marck pendant les années 1789, 1790 et 1791.* (3 Vols, ed. M. A. de Bacourt, Paris, 1891); the *Mémoires* of Malouet (Paris, 1874); and *Correspondance de Maximilien et Augustin Robespierre* (ed. Georges Michon, Paris, 1926, *Société des Études Robespierristes*). Such original sources should be looked at carefully – they reveal how human were the leaders of the Revolution and show how little contemporaries understood the nature of the social changes that were taking place around them. It is easy to forget so simple a point.

R.B.J.

CONTENTS

MAPS

ACKNOWLEDGMENTS

For permission to quote copyright material the author and publishers
wish to thank: Basil Blackwell & Mott Ltd for extracts from *The
French Revolution* by J. M. Thompson; the Clarendon Press, Oxford,
for extracts (including the table reproduced in Appendix 3) from
The Crowd in the French Revolution by George Rudé, and an extract
from *Parisian sans-culottes and the French Revolution* by A. Soboul;
Routledge & Kegan Paul Ltd and Columbia University Press for
extracts from *The French Revolution* (2 vols) by Georges Lefebvre; and
Hutchinson & Co Ltd for the use of *The French Revolution* by A.
Goodwin as a source of various ideas.

PART I
The Background

[1] INTELLECTUAL ORIGINS

The French Revolution ushered in the modern world, for the problems that it posed have been the mainspring of all subsequent political revolutions, and its twin ideals of social equality and 'national self-determination' overthrew the well-ordered world of the eighteenth century. Its impact was the greater because of its dramatic events, and because it happened in France, the leader of European culture.

Europe was then socially very homogeneous: noble and squire had more in common with their own class in other countries than with their own labouring tenants. In almost every capital, the same books and ideas were discussed, and the intelligentsia prided itself upon the debate and experiment that typified their century. The writers and thinkers were called *philosophes*, and their political ideas were widely discussed by the generation preceding the Revolution. Some historians have assigned to them a major part among the causes of the Revolution; but their ideas did not launch it – indeed, had it been only intelligence that threatened the established order of the Ancien Régime, it would have run no risk. Instead, quite independent of the *philosophes*, it was a series of coincidences that gave rise to the Revolution: government bankruptcy, associated with an economic catastrophe, produced a political crisis that overturned the Ancien Régime and brought social and political changes with unprecedented speed. These changes had not been foreseen in any real sense and the Revolution struggled on from crisis to crisis –

Napoleon owed his rise to the resulting chaos. But the chaos is perhaps the measure of the failure of the *philosophes:* their writings were not what Taine called 'the central motor of events'. There was no Lenin to plan the Revolution. Yet *philosophe* ideas inspired revolutionaries then and have done so since.

During the eighteenth century, the reading public greatly increased and by its end it was possible for a writer to live without patronage. Furthermore, the social convention of the aristocratic *salons*, where the *beau monde* met to discuss ideas on a great range of subjects, raised the status and importance of writers. A Voltaire of the 1780s would not have suffered indignities at the hands of a Chevalier de Rohan. But at the beginning of the century, conditions had been hard and censorship by the church, the government and the law courts had been vigorously applied. The *lettre de cachet*, by which the king could imprison a subject without cause shown and without trial, was then a thing to be feared. In consequence, much of the early *philosophe* writing was a literature of protest, demanding freedom of expression and thought. It soon developed into a general attack upon established institutions and a demand for political reforms. Diderot, at the time of Maupeou's coup against the Parlements in 1771 (see page 36), noted that 'Each century has its peculiar spirit ... ours seems to be that of liberty', but he went on to comment shrewdly that this encouraged writers to assume a spirit of revolt against the monarchy that they did not really intend – to demand freedom of thought was not to demand revolution.

The attack was first launched against clerical intolerance and as the century progressed anticlericalism became widespread, while deist views became popular among the upper clergy. The writers were not opposed to religion, and showed a commendable awareness of the social importance of the Church, but the impact of anticlerical writing cannot be over emphasized, for it led naturally to criticism of the arbitrary powers of autocratic government. The *philosophes* often wrote in terms of ideal societies, but the mainspring of their ideas was the political conflicts of the previous century: it was not they who discovered equality of rights or first put forward 'democratic' arguments against arbitrary government, or opposed the 'divine right of kings' by the social contract. Their most influential book, perhaps, was Bayle's *Dictionnaire historique et critique* (1697), a characteristic seventeenth-century work; but by the middle of the century most writers were united in opposing royal absolutism. Their views on government varied; not all of them advocated democracy – Montesquieu, whose *De l'esprit des lois* (1748) was most popular in aristocratic *salons*, was favoured not so much for praising the British constitution, as for proposing a balance between the powers of privileged bodies within the State. His influence is to be seen in the *révolte nobiliaire* (see page 43), not in 1789. Diderot's *l'Encyclopédie*, a compendium of modern knowledge, appeared between 1751 and 1765: it proved critical and even subversive of established institutions and was widely read by the generation preceding the Revolution. Rousseau heralded the Romantic Revival with his two great popular novels, *La nouvelle héloïse* (1760) and *Émile* (1762), but his really original *Du contrat social* (1762) was not widely read before 1789: the influence of his political writings before the Revolution has been grossly exaggerated.

Practical problems of government did not greatly concern the *philosophes* and they scarcely considered the majority of the population, the peasantry, or even the artisans of the towns. They might please liberal nobles and the bourgeoisie by opposing the abuse of arbitrary power and the social privileges of feudalism and demanding a constitution, but it was not to avenge the writers who had once been imprisoned there that the Bastille was stormed, nor was it in response to the *philosophes* that the peasants overthrew feudalism in the summer of 1789. To attribute the development of the Revolution to the writings of the *philosophes* is to accept a counter-revolutionary myth which probably began with Burke.

The writers who prided themselves on their practical ideas were the *physiocrats*, who followed Quesnay. They were interested in what we would call economics and were advocates of the new agricultural methods that were proving so successful in England. They agreed with Adam Smith's free trade views and their principle was laissez-faire, or no government interference with the free and natural functioning of the economic process. Naturally they opposed bureaucratic government, and many of the deputies during the Revolution were inspired by their views – indeed, these were to play an important part in the disputes of the following century. But the majority of peasants rejected their agricultural ideas – and who would claim nineteenth-century capitalism as a *physiocrat* discovery?

The writers' most important achievement was to inspire a general spirit of criticism hostile to existing institutions, and the resulting 'ferment of ideas' heightened the crises of the 1780s. Their views were astonishingly widely diffused (except among the peasantry): many factors helped this diffusion – increased literacy; relaxed censorship; lack of respect for, or fear of, the church and the monarchy; the growth of *salons*, even amongst the petty bourgeoisie; the royal libraries, open throughout the century, extended their hours and sometimes had as many as four hundred readers of an afternoon; newsheets, theatres, cafés and clubs (masonic lodges, introduced from England in 1715, may have played a part) – all these helped to spread reforming ideas. Provincial towns were as active as Paris – in 1789, they had no need to await instructions from the capital. When the Estates General was called, there was a widespread feeling that a new era of national regeneration had arrived – a feeling for which the *philosophes* could claim much credit.

The French government itself took important steps towards the ending of privilege and the enlargement of civil liberty – for example, abolishing the Jewish personal tax (1784) and the important edict of toleration (1787) granting Protestants civil rights. In Europe, 'enlightened despots', especially the Austrian Emperor and the King of Prussia, were indulging in schemes to reform and modernize their countries: ideas of reform were widespread. In the New World, the American Revolution had inspired many volunteers to go and fight for political liberty (though few went to Poland) and France's intervention ensured American success. The volunteers returned, like Lafayette,

ardent advocates of political liberty. '*Imitez les américains*' became a rallying cry in the *salons*; and Jefferson's forthright prose
of the Declaration of Independence echoed through the Old
World. It enshrined the liberty of citizens to choose their own
government, and their right to resist and change a bad one
' . . . it is the right of the people to alter or abolish it, and to insti-
tute new government, laying its foundation on such principles
and organizing its powers in such form as to them shall seem
most likely to effect their safety and happiness'. But the emotion-
al impact of the American War can be exaggerated, however; for
the volunteers, it was effectively over by 1781 – they could
scarcely have maintained their ardour at boiling point throughout the 1780s.

The 'ferment of ideas' did not result in any clear programme
for particular reforms. Nowhere is this better illustrated than in
the statement of grievances (*cahier de doléances*) that the government required from each Estate when the Estates General met in
1789. Censorship was removed to provide for the fullest discussion, and the result was a flood of pamphlets. Perhaps the
most important was Sieyès's *Qu'est-ce que, le Tiers Etat?* – almost
everybody, he answered, and yet nobody, because they were
excluded from government. Yet, though the *cahiers* revealed
some common desires – for instance, to end despotic royal power
and to create a monarchical constitution to replace it – these were
not many. They might repeat catch-phrases from political
writers, but on vital issues each Estate sought to promote its own
interests exclusively. The Church was concerned to defend its
corporate privileges and the nobles to maintain their honorific
rights and feudalism. The bourgeoisie did not need the *philosophes* to teach them to desire an end of social inequality, or to
promote the career open to talent. What could be more telling
than the Paris *cahier: 'Tout citoyen a le droit d'être admis à tous
les emplois, professions et dignités'?*

In August 1789 the famous Declaration of the Rights of Man
and the Citizen, which was to be the preface to the 1791 Constitution, was promulgated. It preserved some over-tones from the
American Declaration (Lafayette had been in communication

with Jefferson) and presented the world with a plain statement
of intention, asserting political equality. Aulard has called it the
death warrant of privilege. Here might be seen *philosophe* ideas
in action, yet it was no abstract formulation, for the deputies had
become well aware of the practical problems of government –
and, in addition, it had become necessary to legalize the revolutionary actions that had already been taken in 1789. The deputies were practical men: they were not dominated by abstract
ideas.

The *philosophes* popularized ideas destructive of the Ancien
Régime, and the leaders of the Revolution – Lafayette, Mirabeau, Danton, Barnave, Roland, Robespierre – were steeped in
these ideas. But there was little agreement on a common policy
for reform. Danton might say, '*La République était dans l'esprit
vingt ans au moins avant sa proclamation*', but many of the
political classes did not applaud its arrival – indeed it was less
proclaimed than forced on France by the king himself, and this
as late as 1792. When it came to an issue, the privileged Orders
fought to retain their privileges and the Third Estate, without
a programme, struggled to control a Revolution whose tremendous power it only dimly realized. The peasant, on whom, in the
last resort, everything depended, for the most part would not
have understood the *philosophes*, and would have been shocked
by their anticlericalism.

The immediate cause of the Revolution was the Crown's bankruptcy and its consequent attempt to reform the administration.
In defence of their privileges, the nobles resisted the attempt and
thus precipitated the Revolution. They could quote Montesquieu
as their justification: 'If, in a monarchy, the prerogatives of the
feudal nobles, clergy, aristocracy and cities are abolished, you will
soon have either a democratic or a despotic state'. It was the
bourgeoisie who completed the Revolution – and profited greatly
from it. But they believed they were promoting justice and
right, not merely for Frenchmen but for humanity. There was
great idealism in the Revolution, for which the *philosophes* can
claim some credit. Those who risked their lives in promoting the
Revolution, who, in the name of universal liberty, declared war

on Europe, who fought at Valmy and at Fleurus, were not men inspired merely by self-interest.

[2] ECONOMIC FACTORS

Some historians, pointing to the extensive agrarian disturbances, have suggested that the Revolution sprang from 'the people' suffering a misery they could no longer bear. Subsequent re-search has put the very real distress of the 1780s into a more subtle perspective. There had been bad years before and were to be again; but these did not precipitate revolutions. The distress of the eighties, coinciding with a political and financial crisis, drove the Revolution into the incipient civil war of the summer of 1789. Economic factors play a vital part in that 'unfavourable concatenation of events' from which the Revolution sprang. In a deeper sense they underlie the political and social desires of particular classes. Furthermore, as always, it was the govern-ment that was blamed for the bad conditions which darkened the atmosphere of discontent with the Ancien Régime.

One must look at developments during the century in order to assess the significance of economic factors, for their importance lies in their long-term effects. An expanding population does not necessarily indicate a rising standard of living, but when associ-ated with an expanding economy it is an important factor in promoting economic growth. From the beginning of the century, Europe witnessed a veritable population explosion and France was the most populous country (this was why she could put so many armies in the field in the 1790s). In 1715, her population was about 18 million, in 1789 about 26 million, of whom only about $2\frac{1}{2}$ million lived in towns. The fall in the death rate (itself in-dicative of a rising standard of living) helps to explain this phen-omenal growth; also, despite numerous economic crises, there was no repetition of the great famine of 1709 – although in 1774 and 1789, farmers had to live on turnips, milk and grass, and day-labourers were very badly off. The population increase was greatest among the rural and urban poor. This meant increased demand for food and land; it meant plenty of surplus labour but also low wages, which in any case tended to lag behind prices, and a greater danger of bread riots in bad years. However, a greater total of money was paid out in wages to day-labourers as a whole, and this total sum could buy more meat, bread, wine, and clothes to provide for the growing population. Increased demand is the parent of increased production. So long as the market held, the increased population tended to act as an accelerator on the economy as a whole. But, if more money was available, this did not mean that everyone was proportionately better off.

The price rise swallowed up much of the extra money. Between 1741 and 1789, prices rose by some 65 per cent, while nominal wages rose by only 22 per cent. There is no clear explanation of this inflationary tendency, although France absorbed about half the precious metal imported into Europe between 1726 and 1780 – in a sense, the march to the Bastille began in the gold and silver mines of Mexico and Peru. More money in circulation meant the expansion of credit facilities and markets, although production did not rise proportionately fast. The price rise affected everyone, but hit hardest those living at subsistence level, the poor artisans and labourers of the towns and the great mass of peasants. The cost of necessities rose steeply and with the pressure of population and shortage of farming land available, rural France faced a serious problem even in good years – yet the population continued to increase and, if they lived miserably, they were better off than their grandparents – indeed, they were the most prosperous peasants on the continent. But in bad years there were always riots and wild rumours were current of hoarders and grain speculators who were growing fat on the misery of the poor, and of a *pacte de famine*, with the government in league with the speculators to hold back the grain to get the highest prices. Such rumours were common throughout the century: they were to mean much in town and country during the Revolution.

Most French merchants were prosperous, and their impatience

with the irksomeness of social privilege increased in proportion to their wealth. During the century industrial production doubled and foreign trade trebled – although, colonial trade apart, Louis XVI's reign saw a slackening in the rate of growth. The great seaports throve and still boast fine eighteenth-century buildings. With ample capital available, a proof of the country's prosperity, merchants were unlikely long to accept the status of second-class citizens.

Industry expanded less than trade, but distilling and sugar refining was important at Bordeaux; Rouen was the centre of a vast cotton industry organized on a domestic scale; and at Lyons, a banking centre and the most magnificent town of the provinces with some 160,000 people, the silk industry had long been established. In textiles new machines were being introduced, although only some 900 jennies were working by 1789 as opposed to 20,000 in England. Heavy industry was expanding and William Wilkinson was managing the blast furnaces of Le Creusot from 1778 to 1781. In 1785 Berthollet had revolutionized bleaching; the Montgolfiers were experimenting with balloons and Lavoisier was laying the foundation of future victories by making French gunpowder the best in the world. French industry was expanding – second only to British by the end of the century.

But nineteenth-century capitalism had not come to eighteenth-century France. Abundant capital was available only in Paris, and most nobles, prepared to invest in merchant adventures, were inhibited from investing in home industries. Despite developments in banking and double-entry book-keeping, business methods were slow to develop – few merchant houses used commercial travellers and few retailers specialized. Internal trade was undeveloped and both manorial and internal customs barriers discouraged inland transport. The government had built fine roads radiating from Paris, but they were for military and administrative purposes, not commercial, and Arthur Young commented on the lack of traffic on them. Nevertheless, France was prosperous and, though the poor may have felt poorer in the 1780s, the Revolution did not spring from a misery 'the people' could no longer bear.

From 1738 to 1815 French wealth grew tremendously, but the rate of growth was not uniform. Periodically there was a slump and, since France was predominantly agricultural, these were always associated with an agricultural crisis. C. E. Labrousse in his important study of French economic history (*La Crise de l'économie française à la fin de l'Ancien Régime et au début de la Révolution*, Presses Universitaires de France, Paris 1943), has shown the peculiar difficulty that Louis XVI's government faced at a time when the idea of a national economy was not even conceived of – but, though the government did not understand it, the problem was central to its difficulties. The Seven Years' War, (1756–63) though a serious defeat for France, was followed by a period of exceptional economic growth until the 1770s. But by 1778 prices were temporarily in decline, and Louis XVI's reign proved to be one of abnormal economic stagnation. This recession lasted until 1787, when a serious drop in production began. Viewed as an incident on a graph, it was no more than the usual cyclical downswing that was to become such a feature of nineteenth-century economy; it was over by 1791, and a period of expansion followed – but by that time the Revolution was a fact. What made this downswing the more dangerous was first, in Labrousse's words, that it 'attacked an organism already very anaemic', and secondly, that it was associated with a particularly severe agricultural crisis that caused prices, especially of the coarser grains, to rise very steeply. A host of unfortunate consequences followed: the peasant had to pay more for his bread and so had less for clothes and other consumer goods; the rural market shrank and textiles were badly hit – cloth production in 1789 was about half that of 1787. Foreign sales were also falling off, and a war in Eastern Europe (see page 80) interrupted trade. It was no wonder that wages fell sharply and that unemployment rose by 50 per cent. The towns felt the depression worse than the countryside. To contemporaries it seemed that the whole economy, undermined by ten years' stagnation was crumbling. Here, rather than in political history, lies the explanation of much of the disturbances in the early years of the Revolution.

The agricultural crisis was caused by a series of disasters. A severe drought and fodder shortage in 1785 meant less livestock and wool – this affected Eastern France especially. There was also a slump in wine sales that meant less money available in the normally profitable wine areas. Rouen had not recovered from a disastrous cotton famine resulting from dislocated trade caused by the British blockade during the Maritime War (1778–83), and this meant less money for peasant families relying on earnings from domestic industry. High prices meant peasants all over France could not afford to buy the usual quantity of seed for sowing. Then, in 1786, the government, more concerned with foreign policy than Free Trade, negotiated the Eden Treaty with Britain, which relieved wine producers but, by lowering tariffs, obliged the textile industry to meet severe competition. This seemed to explain the industry's difficulties and the *cahiers*, understandably, denounced the treaty – and yet it only became fully operative in 1788: it was only natural to lay the blame for economic troubles upon the government. The 1787 harvest was good, but the government, under Loménie de Brienne, allowed free trade in corn and thus emptied the granaries. The wet spring and hailstorms of 1788 ruined the harvest of that year and the government, in the thick of a political crisis produced by its own lack of money, failed to import grain quickly enough. The price of bread – to some extent the gauge of public order – rose steeply and remained high throughout the spring and summer of 1789, taking about three-quarters of a day labourers' wage – if he were lucky enough to be in employment. The most serious shortage would come in mid-summer, before the new harvest was gathered in, when food supplies would have run very low indeed.

With our knowledge of what happened later, we can see that the depression of 1787–91, although it came after a period of stagnation and was accompanied by an abnormally severe agricultural crisis, was only a temporary set-back to a general rise in productivity. France showed her resources of wealth by fighting a war for twenty years – even if much of the expense was borne by her victims. There had been serious economic crises before, but the sudden slump of 1787–9 coincided with a political crisis arising out of the government's lack of money. The

economic background to the Revolution helped to increase the
pressure for social change from the prosperous bourgeoisie, and
temporarily to increase the distress of the great mass of the
people, particularly in the towns, where disorder could confidently be predicted. The extended recession had sadly reduced the
government's financial resources at the very time it was most
seriously under pressure. Without the political crisis there would
have been no Revolution, for its parent was not distress; but the
prevailing economic conditions explain much of the course that
the Revolution took.

[3] FRENCH SOCIETY

Behind the political crisis there lay also the social problem.
Under the Ancien Régime, French Society was divided into three
broad Estates or Orders. It was possible to move between them,
but it was becoming progressively more difficult; indeed the
nobles seemed to wish to make themselves into a caste. The cohesion of British and American society did not exist in France –
Turgot complained that it was 'mal-unis'. Both within classes
and between them there was what Cournot called a 'cascade of
scorn' for those in a lower position and the mutual hostility that
resulted impeded the growth of a society more suited to prevailing
economic conditions.

The broad division into three Estates concealed a complex
social structure about which it is dangerous to generalize. The
First Estate, the clergy, claimed an ultimate precedence and,
despite political disputes between Gallican and Ultramontane,
admitted only the Pope as their head. There were some 180,000
clergy and they pervaded the social life of the community. They
were not a class but an Order with their own courts and assemblies and an exclusive right to tax themselves – the Church
Assembly would vote a 'don gratuit' to the King, which was
usually financed by Paris bankers. The Church had always pro-

vided an avenue of promotion for bright young men, but higher clerical offices went increasingly to younger sons of nobles. In 1789 all the 143 bishops were nobles, most of whom lived at court and rarely visited their dioceses, and the lucrative posts of abbot, prior and canon were mostly held by nobles too. The great wealth of the higher clergy was a favourite object of attack by anti-clerical writers, as also was the dissolute behaviour of some bishops, like the Cardinal de Rohan, chiefly remembered for his part in the Diamond Necklace scandal, or the brilliant Talleyrand. Below these came the bookish young men, often of bourgeois origin, the cathedral chapters and seminary teachers (men like Fouché or Sieyès), who saw their chances of a bishopric, the head of an abbey, or other such posts, now almost reserved for nobles, fade as the century progressed. A long way below these were the simple parish *curés*, some men with a calling, others as ignorant as their flock, but all miserably poor – although the stipend (*portion congrue*) was raised in 1786 to 700 livres for *curés* and 350 for *vicaires*. Many were envious of the wealth of their superiors and this caused a rift in clerical ranks that was to be of supreme importance in 1789. But it would be a great mistake to dismiss the clergy as worldly and indifferent to their spiritual duties, or to suppose that, because the anticlerical *philosophes* were so popular, religion was in eclipse. It was more than politics that led so many upper clergy as well as *curés*, to oppose the Civil Constitution of 1790 (see page 67) and to continue their ministry despite persecution as counter-revolutionaries.

The Second Estate was composed of some 400,000 nobles headed by the Princes of the Blood. Deeply conscious of their status and privileges, there was little unity among them – Talleyrand commented '*Au lieu d'une noblesse, il y en avait sept ou huit*'. There was a very small number of *noblesse d'épée*, proud descendants of ancient feudal families; then came the *noblesse de robe*, families that had acquired noble status through purchase of offices in the Parlements, law courts or administration. Many of these were very wealthy. And there was also the *anoblis*, who had purchased letters of nobility. The contempt felt by the older

nobility for the new lessened during the century as ancient
families shored up their fortunes with a wealthy marriage – some
even married in plebeian circles. As an Order they were exempt
from direct taxes except for the *vingtième* and capitation tax,
and even here they generally made a good bargain with the tax
farmer. Their social privileges were considerable, and seigneurial
and hunting rights, sometimes personal servitude, survived,
quite apart from their feudal dues. Louis-Sébastien Mercier
paints a savage picture of the behaviour of fashionable nobles
in his *Tableau de Paris* (1783); a heavy gambling debt would be
repaid as a matter of honour, but let tradesmen demand payment – '*Les impertinents! Qu'on aille chez d'autres. Je leur retire
ma protection*'. And a noble newly ennobled would be more noble
than any! If a noble fell foul of the law, special courts tried him –
and he could not be hanged or whipped, for this happened to
commoners only. It is small wonder that the Declaration of
Rights should proclaim equality before the law and the career
open to talent (Article 6) and a fair tax system (Article 13).

As with the clergy, wealth underlined an important social
division between rich and poor. The former, the *noblesse de cour*,
lived at Versailles, where extravagance led them into financial
difficulties. Many received sinecures and honours; if they were
friendly with the queen, they were lucky – like the Polignacs.
But costs were high: the Duc d'Orléans, the greatest landowner
in France, contracted debts of 74,000,000 livres. Sometimes,
indeed, the issue of a *lettre de cachet* confining a riotous son to his
estates was welcomed as much as a means of controlling him, as
of saving money. (By Louis XVI's reign, the days had passed
when the *lettre de catchet* was a dread instrument of royal despotism.) Some nobles invested in merchant companies, others promoted industry, like de Croy with his Anzin coal interests, the
Duc d'Orléans built apartment houses at the Palais-Royal and
Talleyrand was well known on the Bourse. But these were the
exceptions; as a whole they did not share the taste of the
English noble for agriculture and commerce.

In the provinces lived the impoverished nobles, intensely
aware of their position and bitterly jealous and scornful of their

wealthier bourgeois neighbours. Sometimes they ploughed their own fields, or, as Tocqueville shows, carried their wares to market dressed like their peasants, but always carrying their sword as a sign of their class. The Marquis de Bouillé spoke of their resembling ancient oaks '*mutilés par le temps, dont il ne reste que le tronc dépouillé*'. The great nobles, whom they envied, could toy with new ideas, even experiment with new agricultural methods, but they needed their status and they depended on their feudal dues both as a source of much needed capital and as a guarantee of their social superiority – nor would they lose caste (*déroger*) by engaging in commerce and industry. From the provincial nobles came the greatest resistance to change. Yet this picture is too simple, for local studies have revealed the existence of some enterprizing businesslike nobles (see, for example, R. Forster's *The Nobility of Toulouse in the Eighteenth Century*, Johns Hopkins University Studies in Historical and Political Science, Series LXXVIII, No. 1, 1960).

In the generation before the Revolution, the nobles had come to a greater awareness of their common interests – in due course they were to present a united front to the king. During Louis XVI's reign there was a determined effort to regain the political power from which Richelieu and Louis XIV had excluded them. An extensive aristocratic literature flourished, like Comte de Boulainvillier's account of their descent from the conquering Franks. Their exclusiveness grew and their pressure on the high offices of state raised a barrier against the bourgeoisie. By the 1750s the purchase of ennobling office was not easy and proof of noble birth had become a requirement for many posts. Of the thirty-six ministers with portfolios between 1774 and 1789, only Necker was not a noble – and his daughter became Mme de Staël, a baroness and 'Mistress of an Age'. All bishops were nobles in 1789, so were many lesser ecclesiastics, so were the household officers about the royal family, and the intendants. In 1781, the famous Ségur ordinance reserved army commissions to men of noble birth. The climax came with the political crisis of 1786-8 (see pages 43-4) when there was close cooperation between the Provincial Estates, dominated by older nobility, and the Parle-

ments, strong-hold of the *noblesse de robe*, to resist any encroachment on their privileges. Here was a determined aristocratic reaction that blocked avenues of promotion to the bourgeoisie,
heightened the resentment of the unprivileged and culminated
in revolt against royal authority.

As more is discovered about the social history of the Ancien
Régime, generalizations become less satisfactory. This is especially true of the Third Estate. It was everyone not in the other
two Estates – some 96 per cent of the population, according to
Sieyès. There were perhaps a million bourgeois and some 23
million peasants and urban workers. All lacked the customary
privileges enjoyed by the clergy and the nobility. The bourgeoisie were perhaps the best educated and wealthiest group in
France – and they managed to avoid some of the direct taxation
to which they were normally liable. They were divided into two
groups: the upper bourgeois, who tended to slip into the nobility
if he could acquire an appropriate office, was a professional man,
a wealthy civil servant (probably having bought a 'venal'
office) or an important merchant or banker. They were a small
group, as exclusive as the nobles, whose prestige they resented.
The lower, or petty, bourgeoisie was less well defined; they were
the less prosperous merchants and lawyers, writers and apothe-
caries and some master-craftsmen and shop-keepers. Between
the two there was that antagonism that is visible today: yet the
petty bourgeois was scornful of those beneath him – Mme Lebas,
daughter of the contractor Duplay, who let rooms to Robespierre,
maintained that her father would have compromised his dignity
had he invited one of his labourers to sup with him.

As avenues of promotion closed, some complained that the
sacrifices they had made to provide their sons with a good
education met with but small reward – Brissot, Danton, Vergniaud are good examples. 'The road is blocked in all directions',
wrote Joseph Barnave. Conscious of their ability and superiority to most nobles, they felt themselves humiliated. Of course
they wanted the career open to talent. Many had endeavoured
to 'prove' themselves nobles, like Carnot and the Rolands –
indeed there existed lawyers' firms that specialized in 'verifying'

family trees. Robespierre, as Secretary of the Assembly, signed the decree abolishing titles of nobility (1790) with the 'de' he had used before the Revolution; Brissot, son of a Chartres inn-keeper, called himself Brissot de Ouarville. They were made conscious of their inferior status; Barnave became a revolutionary when a noble turned his mother out of a box at the Grenoble theatre; and when Mme Roland was asked to dinner at the Château de Fontenay, she was served in the servants' hall. Injured pride led many to a hatred of the nobility and the Ancien Régime.

In the towns the proletariat was the lowest class, condemned as manual labourers to an inferior level of civilization by nobles and bourgeoisie alike. They did not present the threat of a 'red peril' (had they done, the Girondins and Jacobins would have acted very differently) for they were numerous only in Paris and Lyons: for the most part, since they produced no *jacquerie* such as the peasants threatened, their fate was ignored by the Revolution. They have been ignored, too, by many historians, except to be classed variously as 'the people' or 'the mob'. More recent studies, penetrating beneath the surface of purely political history, have shown how infinitely complex were the groups that made up the working classes of the towns. Day labourers and journeymen were unorganized, although the *compagnonnes* in the building trade had extensive links with many towns and struck for higher wages from time to time. Efforts to organize journeymen and to use the strike weapon were met by repression at the hands of master-craftsmen in the guilds and by the police – like the famous Lyons strike of 1785, at which the language of nineteenth-century labour agitators was heard. Even in Paris, with the unemployment and hunger of 1789, there was little sign of workers' solidarity. The only truly insurrectionary movement of wage earners in Paris in 1789 was the Réveillon riot of 27 April, a peculiar incident that took everyone by surprise and was suppressed by the military.

But midway between what could be called working class and the petty bourgeoisie come a group about which it is particularly dangerous to generalize: the *sans-culottes*. Professor George Rudé (*The Crowd in the French Revolution*, Oxford University

Press, 1959) has shown that the famous mob, which Taine called '*la dernière plèbe* . . . *d'une physionomie effrayante*', was in fact led and given cohesion by the *sans-culottes*. As the Revolution progressed, the Third Estate, at first united in mutual hostility against privilege, disintegrated into separate conflicting groups. In the towns, and especially in Paris, the small shopkeepers, superior artisans and some journalists gradually exerted an influence that was to bring them into conflict with the bourgeoisie and to explain much of the political crisis which marked the fall of the Girondins, and the launching of the Great Terror in September 1793. They were distinguished by their dress: trousers were worn by the workers, not the knee-breeches (*culottes*) of the richer lawyers. Robespierre, who in some ways came to be their leader, contrasted the '*culottes dorées*' of the rich with the trousers of the *sans-culottes*. It was a symbol of their egalitarian outlook, for they were resentful of 'rank-pulling'. They were distinguished by a social antagonism, too, for they regarded themselves as virtuous poor and the wealthy as likely to be corrupt and 'aristocratic' (a word which for them came to mean anyone against the Revolution). There was certainly a strain of puritanism in their outlook, and also a hatred of wastrels and parasites. It is ironic that the shopkeepers, the very class that one thinks of as conformist and on the side of the police, should be the class that, wielding power through the Paris Sections, should overthrow the Girondins and bring in the Terror. Some have seen in them the urban proletariat of Marx, but they had little social philosophy beyond distrust of the wealthy and a desire to reinforce the price control efforts of the Ancien Régime to keep down the price of bread. Hostility towards privilege at the beginning of the Revolution concealed the mutual hostility within the urban classes between bourgeoisie and *sans-culottes*. It became more pronounced as the Revolution progressed and came to the surface for the first time clearly in the massacre of the Champ de Mars in July 1791 (see page 77).

[4] THE PEASANTS

Formerly historians regarded the peasant as dutifully waiting upon political events in Paris; indeed, he scarcely appears in many histories. This is odd, because there were some 23 million peasants out of a total population of 26 million Frenchmen. History is not made by individual leaders alone. In fact, the peasant continued a revolution all his own, which touched the main current of the Revolution from time to time. The complexities and great regional variations within the peasant class have been revealed by modern historians (see especially Lefebvre's *Études sur la Révolution française*, Presses Universitaires de France, 1954).

The peasants were the backbone of France; any government depended on their tacit consent. Yet their grievances over taxation and feudalism were well known: cartoons of the 1780s show the peasant struggling to carry the weight of national taxes and to support clergy and noble as well. He was the beast of burden, and despite the interest in simple rural pleasures which came with the popularity of Rousseau's novels, the privileged and bourgeois classes did not *really* think of him as an equal human being. The clergy exacted the great tithe, most of which went to indifferent bishops, abbeys or cathedral chapters, or even to lay landlords, to whom it had been 'sub-infeudated', and the small tithe, some of which might go to the curé, besides other payments for specific services. Tithes were a considerable burden usually being paid in kind, though they varied between regions. Direct taxation was even more of a burden, the king levying a poll tax, *vingtième*, and a *taille*, which, since it was based on external evidence of wealth, meant that the peasant concealed his money and lived in poverty to deceive the tax-gatherer. Rousseau tells of his difficulty in begging a crust of bread, for, being a stranger, he was suspected of being a spy. The peasant had to pay the *gabelle* (salt tax), which the *gabelous* were severe in extorting, he was subject to the *corvée* (forced labour on public

works) or had to pay a tax in lieu, his cart might be commandeered for transporting military supplies and, if unmarried, he
had to draw lots for military service. As costs rose, royal demands
increased – yet the peasant survived and was often not so poor as
he seemed; nor was he opposed to the monarchy.

Feudal servitude, surviving as a social and economic burden,
was hated – yet it was less burdensome than elsewhere on the
Continent. Only a few serfs were to be found in Eastern France,
but they were no longer tied to the soil and Louis XVI had
abolished the right of pursuit in 1779. For the most part the
peasant was free and owned land, yet the lord claimed an 'emi-
nent' right over it exacting an annual *cens* or quit-rent and heavy
lods et ventes, dues on inheritance and sale. Many tolls (*péages*)
were no longer charged, but there remained many local dues in
money and in kind. If the peasant challenged the legal right to
feudal charges (and he did) his appeal from the seigneurial court
lay to the superior courts and *Parlements*, where the right was
generally upheld. Apart from 'real' rights, the lord exacted
banalités – the compulsory use of his mill, bakery, wine-press,
etc. In some areas he had hunting rights (*capitaineries*) and he
maintained a rabbit warren and a *colombier* for doves and
pigeons regardless of damage to his peasant's crops. Many lords,
too, were encroaching on their peasants' common rights. Bailiffs
of absentee lords were generally accused of particular severity
in applying rights. Furthermore, many lords realized that it was
profitable to farm out certain rights to capitalists, and the
peasants suffered in consequence – for instance, in the hands of
wholesale Lorraine butchers, the *droit de troupeau à part* (the
lord's right to graze his herds separately from village cattle)
meant vast herds grazing on land the lord would have left to the
peasants' cattle.

The pattern of land tenure was very different from that then
emerging in Britain. The clergy held probably 10 per cent of the
kingdom (much of it wealthy urban property), the nobles about
25 per cent, with extensive holdings in Brittany, but much less
elsewhere, as in the Auvergne. The bourgeoisie held perhaps
20 per cent, usually near towns, the peasant about 35 per cent,

but with vast regional differences – around Versailles 75 per cent of the families held no land, in Limousin perhaps 50 per cent, in the north east about 20 per cent. Peasant land ownership was increasing – a sign of growing wealth. But many holdings were too small: in the fertile north east, Lefebvre calculated that a family needed 5 hectares, yet in Cambrésis 70 per cent held less than one and 20 per cent less than 5 hectares. This was common throughout France, and it was aggravated both by the growing population and the custom of dividing holdings between sons. By the end of the century there was land hunger – but it did not compare with that in Eastern Europe and the peasants' revolt did not arise from this factor alone.

Occasionally one could find a wealthy peasant, owning or renting a large farm, scarcely to be distinguished from the local squire. Everywhere there was a small group of *laboureurs* each owning or renting a farm big enough to support his family. Then came the great mass of the rural proletariat, each with a cottage and garden, perhaps a strip or small field, or land leased on a share-cropping (*métayage*) basis, and frequently dependent on wages as a day labourer. They were increasing because of the population growth and the multiplication of holdings, and in several areas cottage industry was essential to supplement income. National wealth was growing, but there was always plenty of rural distress. Many families migrated in search of work at harvest and grape-picking time: in bad years they became vagrants – a persistent nuisance, for poor relief was ill organized.

Most families lived near to poverty, with insufficient land for their needs, so it was vital for peasants to maintain their common rights, like pasturage and gleaning after harvest – labourers used the sickle in preference to the scythe, for it made gleaning more profitable. A part of the unpopularity of the tithe was that it took away straw as well as grain. Producing for subsistence only, from small holdings, with little money for improvements or experimenting with new crops and methods, even if they were interested in them, the peasant was a powerful force maintaining primitive traditional methods. Enclosure of commons and attempts to consolidate holdings were violently opposed – a sub-

stantial boycott developed in Picardy. In a phrase, the peasant
opposed the agricultural revolution – successfully. Even so, the
picture is once again too simple, for there did exist peasants
wealthy enough to experiment with innovations.

New methods were discussed. The *physiocrats* promoted them
and royal administrators dreamed of great reforms increasing
production and trade – but they shrank from the daunting consequences of pursuing an active policy. Instead they promoted
agricultural societies that won the extravagant praise of Arthur
Young – yet royal encouragement for the reclaiming of land
scarcely increased productive acreage in thirty years. Unlike
the English, there were too few active and rich landowners
prepared to try new methods. The efforts, especially of the 1780s,
to consolidate holdings in place of share-cropping, to enclose
commons and drive the peasant from the forests (especially as
the price of timber soared), were promoted not by theoreticians,
but by men anxious to augment their incomes to meet the price
rise that hit rich as well as poor, noble as well as peasant. These
efforts have been lumped together under the name of the 'feudal
reaction', and with this, economic, social and political history
come together: it plays a great part in the peasant's revolt.

There were two parts to the feudal reaction: the first was the
intrusion of what we would call capitalist ideas, often under
cover of feudal rights. Enclosure and the 'farming out' of feudal
rights were really the beginnings of the agricultural revolution:
the peasant saw them as an abuse of feudalism, and was determined to end the system. But, properly 'farmed', the feudal
rights were valuable and the provincial nobles were determined
to maintain them and to increase their revenue from them. To
keep the rights meant keeping the existing system of agriculture;
in a sense, the feudal rights were a guarantee that the French
peasant would escape the fate that had overtaken the English
labourer. No peasant – and no noble either – realized this:
instead they adopted positions of mutual antagonism.

The second part of the feudal reaction was the attempt to
increase the revenue from the dues by revising the registers
(*terriers*). Landlords were concerned with income; they were not

agricultural improvers. As early as 1776, Turgot had promoted
Boncerf's '*Les inconvénients des droits feodaux*', but *physiocrat*
views made little progress. As costs rose, greater attention was
paid to all forms of seigneurial dues – which helps to explain the
violent hostility in some areas to the *banalités*. There was nothing
new in revising the *terriers*, but a significant renewal took place
in many areas during the 1780s. Existing dues were increased and
others 'resumed' – specialists in feudal law (*feudistes*) were employed and some earned a commission on their 'discoveries' of
obsolete dues (it was as a *feudiste* that Babeuf, perhaps the first
modern communist, learnt his distrust of property). Royal agents
brought the royal *cens* 'up to date' by an appreciable increase
through the Order of 20 August 1786, for the government
suffered from the price rise, like everyone else. The leasing of
revised feudal dues to 'farmers-general' was very profitable for
it assured the noble of a definite income, but the peasant
suffered, his hatred of feudalism growing. Wherever the 'reaction'
had not occurred, as in La Vendée, where the *terriers* were renewed by custom at the same rate, and so got lighter as prices
rose, there was little hostility between lord and peasant. But this
was the exception: elsewhere the 'reaction' made feudalism the
more onerous and, in conjunction with the serious economic
crisis, made a violent outbreak the more likely. The political
crisis of 1788–9 and the decision to call an Estates General, gave
direction to popular unrest and the hope that things would change
for the better. An old woman in Champagne told Arthur Young:
'It was said that something was to be done by some great folks
for such poor ones, but she did not know who or how, but God
send us better, *car les tailles et les droits nous écrasent*'.

The compilation of the *cahiers* increased the peasant's belief
that his grievances were to be met – even if his 'authentic voice'
was rarely heeded at the local meetings which drew up the
primary *cahiers* (see page 48). But more than *cahiers* were
needed: families were hungry, everywhere food was short and
costly and grain transports were stopped by rioters. Already the
usual rumours of a *pacte de famine* were current. In the spring of
1789 predictable peasant riots occurred, but the peasants were

also declaring their intention of not paying feudal dues: at the same time, and without any prompting, wild rumours of an 'aristocratic plot' to rob the 'people' of their 'revolution', and to reinforce manorial dues, were as widespread in the countryside as in the towns. Such rumours were to play an important part in the Revolution. They seemed to be confirmed by the Estates General's inactivity on the peasant question. Impatience at what must have seemed a betrayal brought the disturbances of the spring to a culmination in a real peasants' revolt in July. The revolt was spontaneous and unorganized: and it was to have tremendous consequences (see pages 55–7).

[5] THE ADMINISTRATION AND THE KING

Much has been made of the despotism of the Bourbons. In fact, despite the work of Richelieu, even Louis XIV's power was checked by legal barriers. It is true that he could claim absolute power because of his position and of the centralized bureaucracy working through the intendants, the royal agents in each Province; but this centralization was more theoretical than real. His successors' attempts to reform it were prevented by those very checks that the Great Monarch had not removed.

The first check to royal authority was the Church, its spiritual influence supported by considerable temporal endowments. With its corporate organization and quinqennial councils that voted '*dons gratuits*' to the king in place of taxation, it was well placed to resist any encroachment on its privileges. The second check was the thirteen ancient high courts of appeal, the Parlements. The Parlement of Paris had acquired the right to register royal decrees, which gave it a potentially powerful position – but it did not fail to register Louis XIV's edicts! The king could enforce his wishes against the Parlement by a *lit de justice*, or by issuing *lettres de cachet* exiling the magistrates to remote villages, or imprisoning them until they 'saw reason'. Louis XV's recourse to such methods enabled the Parlements to pose until 1788 as the

defenders of 'constitutionalism' against a despotic monarchy –
and the agitation they provoked, which was really to maintain
their privileges, gave a topical significance to the writings of the
philosophes.

The third check was the complexity of the administration
itself, arising out of the confusion of feudal survivals. The king
fully controlled the central provinces, the *pays d'élection* – but
the princes of Alsace owed an allegiance also to the Emperor, a
fact that was to be of importance in the dispute over the revoca-
tion of feudal rights. But there were *pays d'état*, provinces added
later to France, having a special relationship to the king, some of
them still retaining a provincial assembly that had a voice in the
administration of the province – e.g. Brittany and Languedoc.
The royal intendant's authority, unchallenged in the *pays
d'élections*, was sometimes checked in the *pays d'état*, which clung
to their privileges – especially those over taxation. John Law was
not quite right when he told the Marquis d'Argenson in 1720,
'*Sachez que ce royaume de France est gouverné par trente Intendants*'.

The famous Bourbon centralized bureaucracy was not, after
all, so streamlined. Beneath it lay a crazy pavement of differing
jurisdictions, varying codes of law and weights and measures.
Its complexities were augmented by the tax system. Considerable
potential revenue was lost to the crown by the clerical and noble
exemption from, and the noble and bourgeois evasion of direct
taxation. Only by wholesale destruction of privilege and the
formal taxing of the clergy, could the yield from direct taxes be
increased. Indirect taxes, on liquor, tobacco, stamp duties, the
gabelle, etc., were 'farmed out' to financiers who took a lease on
the product of the tax and grew prosperous by vigorously collect-
ing it – they probably gained from the price rise, since the Treasury could increase the lease only when it fell vacant after a fixed
period. Such a system could be replaced only by employing a
proper civil service, which would not only be expensive, but
might prove impossible in eighteenth-century conditions. The
government was seriously embarrassed: the price rise meant that
costs rose more steeply than receipts; the court was extravagant,

and the American War alone cost some 2,000 million livres. The current deficit was met by borrowing so that, by 1788, the interest charge on the public debt accounted for 318 million out of a total state expenditure of 630 million livres. Financial reform was necessary before the American War: after it, it was vital. But it could be achieved only at the cost of great social and political changes: it was the attempt to achieve reform that precipitated the Revolution. It did so because of the lack of royal authority, for there was no Henry IV or Louis XIV: yet even so strong a monarch could have succeeded only by facing a most dangerous political crisis.

The institution of monarchy was popular enough. Louis XV, however, had become personally most unpopular: this can be gauged by the number of masses paid for by Parisians when he was ill – in 1744 there had been 6,000; in 1757, 600; in 1774, 3. He has had a bad press, for he was by no means the vicious and indifferent character of popular legend. He had a streak of the real monarch in him; but the tiresome details of public affairs bored him and he preferred court intrigue, his personal 'secret' diplomacy, his women and his hunting. This was not unusual in a king; but Louis XV was associated with extravagance and unsuccessful wars, furthermore he ended his reign with an attack on privilege. The Parlement of Paris was determined to maintain its privileges – '*toute institution nouvelle lui paraissait un acte de rébellion*', Mme de Staël was later to write. Exasperated at its obstructiveness, on the advice of Maupeou, Louis effected a *coup d'état* in 1771, issuing *lettres de cachet* exiling the magistrates to remote villages in Auvergne. The reaction was violent and Louis was widely represented as a despot: but Maupeou proceeded with a series of reforms which his secretary, Lebrun, was to see finally carried out under Napoleon. Louis's sudden death in 1774 brought Maupeou's schemes to restore royal power to an end, for the inexperienced Louis XVI replaced him and restored the Parlements. Ironically, Mme de Staël records that Louis XV wrote to the Duchesse de Choiseul: '*J'ai eu bien de la peine à me tirer d'affaire avec les parlements, pendant mon regne; mais que mon petit-fils* [Louis XVI] *y prenne garde, ils pourraient bien*

mettre sa couronne en danger'. One might almost say it was the
recalling of the Parlement in 1774 which led Louis XVI to the
guillotine in 1793!

The popular welcome to the new king, after the scenes at
Louis XV's funeral, showed that monarchy retained its hold over
popular sentiment: republicanism was still a thing of the future.
But Louis XVI was not a great king: kindly, devout, no lady's
man, bored with politics, sleeping at Council, he was more interested in clocks and in his passion for food and the chase. Royalists were to make much of his sincere Roman Catholicism, but
in the prevailing condition of the Church he could scarcely be
expected to protect it, even had he the capacity to do so. He was
possessed of a curious apathy on political questions, even in the
face of a serious crisis; and yet he was to display strength and
determination during the Revolution, as well as a surprising
capacity for subterfuge. He was also to show both weakness and
strength at just the wrong moments. He lacked political judge-
ment, but was not the weak, well-intentioned innocent of
royalist legend: Joseph II, of Austria, his brother-in-law, commented in 1777, *'cet homme est un peu faible, mais point imbécile'*.
Politically immature, he was often the victim of court intrigues
many of which were to have grave effects upon the course of the
Revolution. Great events often spring from petty causes. Much
of the intrigue centred on the queen, Marie-Antoinette, whom the
king came to regard as his principal councillor, and whose advice
was almost invariably bad.

At first a neglected wife, the queen was in the van of fashion,
whether it was sporting monstrous feather head-dresses, or playing the milk maid; and there gathered around her a group of idle
favourites, like the irresponsible Polignacs and the handsome
young Swede, Count Fersen, who was probably her lover. Her
mother, the great Maria Theresa of Austria, cautioned her, but
to no effect. From the beginning she had a hard task to achieve
popularity, for she was the symbol of the unpopular Austrian
alliance. She was blamed for the extravagance of the court and
by the 1780s she had acquired the nickname *'Madame Déficit'*.
Yet she disliked the strict etiquette of the court, preferring a

narrow group of favourites gathered at the Petit Trianon. Not
only did this cause jealousy, but it led nobles to frequent their
Paris mansions in preference to Versailles, and the court became
increasingly isolated not only from the ordinary people, but from
the mass of the aristocracy. In due course, the Revolution was to
take its revenge on the whole court. But the attack was first
launched by jealous and irresponsible courtiers – perhaps hoping
to bastardize the queen's children and so secure the succession for
Louis's brother, Provence. The Duc d'Orléans, whom royalists
cast for the villain of the piece, was certainly active in the campaign to undermine Louis's position. Scurrilous rumours reached
a peak in 1785 with the infamous Diamond Necklace Scandal,
when a public trial dragged the queen's name in the dirt. It was
not that she was mainly innocent; what mattered was that she
was believed to be so free with her favours. For contemporaries,
what is important is not what happened, but what people are
prepared to believe happened. The mint at Strasbourg struck
several *louis d'ors* with the king's head surmounted by a cuckold's
horn.

While the court, heedless of the consequences, were under-
mining the social authority of the monarch, some of the king's
ministers were endeavouring to reform the administration. But
Turgot, the Controller General of 1774, had to face the recalled
Parlement. Financiers feared for their monopolies, and when, in
1776, he suggested a series of reforms, the Parlement resisted
and Louis replaced him in response to court pressure. From 1776
to 1781, Necker, a protestant banker and millionaire, was in
charge of finance. His great contemporary reputation as a reformer, which he did so much to promote, is no longer accepted;
but at least he saved the situation temporarily by the simple expedient of borrowing – the famous *Compte Rendu* of 1781, a sort
of budget statement, was designed to attract investment. It
completely misrepresented the state of finances, but since the
whole administrative structure was so complicated, Necker may
not have been aware that there was already a very serious running deficit. In 1774, Turgot had warned the king that '*le premier
coup de canon forcerait l'État à la banqueroute*'' yet in 1778 France

entered the American War. To pay for it Necker had to raise
loans at as much as 10 per cent – half the expenditure of the
1780s went on debt redemption. It was fortunate perhaps, for
his reputation as a reformer, that intrigue caused the king to
dismiss him in 1781.

Calonne was the next reformer. He precipitated the crisis
that led to the Revolution. His reputation was besmirched so
much by his enemies that historians are only just realizing what
a good minister he might have been in happier circumstances.
He was Controller General in 1783, but it was not until 1786 that
he really understood the gravity of the situation – it had taken
him so long to discover that as early as 1769 the annual deficit
had been 70 million livres. It was the government that lacked
money, (there was no question of France as a whole being bankrupt), but the administration could be saved from bankruptcy
only by thorough-going reform. The diplomatic consequences of
the crown's lack of money were plain for all to see during the
Dutch crisis of 1787–8 (see page 80), when it could not afford a
mobilization against Prussia, and so saw its interests overturned.

In August 1786 Calonne laid radical, if not highly original
plans of reform before the king, plans that would have saved the
monarchy, but which shrewdly undermined privilege. Twenty
years in the administration, in which whole provinces were
strangers to each other, had convinced Calonne that the whole
political structure of the Ancien Régime would have to be re-
modelled. Anticipating that the Parlement would wreck his
scheme, as it had that of Turgot in 1776, he asked the king to
summon an Assembly of Notables, nominated by the king – to
call the Estates General would be to admit bankruptcy as well as
to introduce the Third Estate into affairs of government. An
Assembly of Notables would not infringe the royal prerogative
and, if it accepted reforms, the Parlement of Paris could scarcely
refuse to register them. Even so, it took a long time to persuade
Louis to call the Notables – evidence of that indecision that was
to trouble the monarch further. Calonne was sanguine enough to
think he could persuade the Notables to tax themselves – despite
the campaign that Necker and his friends were conducting

against him. The futility of this hope was only too well demonstrated by the violent political crisis to which it gave rise. It was
this that precipitated the Revolution. And so one could say that,
when the Assembly of Notables met at Versailles on 22 February
1787, the French Revolution had begun. Not many years later,
Barnave, who although he was embroiled in it, wrote a shrewd
history of the Revolution, commented that the aristocracy had
provoked *'une révolution, dont elle est devenue la victime'*.

Further Reading

The general histories and contemporary writings referred to in
the Preface should be consulted for each relevant section of this
book. An excellent account by an outstanding nineteenth-century historian of social institutions is given in Alexis de Tocqueville's *L'Ancien Régime* (translated by M. W. Patterson,
Blackwell, 1947); it is to be supplemented by, for example,
Alfred Cobban's *A History of Modern France*, Vol. 1 (Penguin,
1963) and John Lough's *An Introduction to Eighteenth-Century
France* (Longmans, 1960). For the *philosophes*, A. Mornet's *Les
Origines intellectuelles de la Révolution Française 1715 to 1787*
(Armand Colin, 1933), and K. Martin's *French Liberal Thought
in the Eighteenth-Century* (Turnstile Press, 1954), are invaluable.
For the influence of Rousseau an important book is Joan Mc-
Donald's *Rousseau and the French Revolution* (Athlone Press,
1966): it corrects some common misunderstandings. A. Cobban's
In Search of Humanity (Cape, 1960) is thought-provoking, and his
Debate on the French Revolution (2nd. ed., Black, 1963), extracts
from contemporary writings, is well worth reading. Lord Elton's
The Revolutionary Idea in France, 1789 to 1871 (Arnold, reprinted
1959) suggests some interesting lines, especially on the revolutionary tradition in the nineteenth century. An important article
on Calonne, by A. Goodwin, is in *English Historical Review*, 1946,
and a helpful article on the peasants, by Alun Davies, appears in
History, Vol XLIX, 1964. An excellent survey of the whole
revolutionary period is provided by Norman Hampson's *Social
History of the French Revolution* (Routledge, 1963).

Principal Events, 1770 – May 1789

FRANCE

1770–4. Ministry of Maupeou

1771. *Coup d'état* against the Parlement. Magistrates exiled to Auvergne.

1774. Accession of Louis XVI; recall of Parlement

1774–6. Turgot's Ministry

1776. American Declaration of Independence

1777–81. Necker in charge of finances

1778. Intervention in American War. 'National' economy stagnates for a decade before the slump of 1787–91

1781. *Compte Rendu*. Necker dismissed
Fall of Yorktown

1783. Treaty of Versailles ends the American War
Calonne Controller General

1785. Diamond Necklace Scandal
Severe forage shortage

1786. Eden (Trade) Treaty. Decision to call Notables

1787. Assembly of Notables
Calonne replaced by Loménie de Brienne
Free trade in corn allowed
Edict of Toleration for Protestants

1787–8. Failure of French diplomacy in Holland

1788. Hailstorms destroy the harvest – food shortage for 1789
Resignation of Brienne and recall of Necker
Decision to call Estates General

1789. Sieyès's *'Qu'est-ce que, le Tiers État?'*
Bread riots in spring and summer; peasant unrest widespread
May. Estates General meet at Versailles

PART II
The First Phase: 1787-9

[6] THE VICTORY OF THE NOTABLES

Calonne may have mishandled the Notables, but they refused to surrender their privileged position. Changes to enhance their position were acceptable: changes that tended towards egalitarianism were not. The king's only recourse now, short of despotism, was to appeal to the bourgeoisie against privilege: as Chateaubriand put it, '*les patriciens commencèrent la révolution, les plébéiens l'achèverent*'. Many modern historians date the beginning of the Revolution from this revolt of the nobility; but some do not agree. Professor Rudé, for instance, argues for a later date (see *Past and Present*, November 1955). Calonne had bitter personal enemies at court (in the person of the queen's favourite, Breteuil, especially) and in the Assembly (notably Loménie de Brienne, Archbishop of Toulouse, who sought to replace him as first minister). It was court intrigue that secured his dismissal in April 1788. The Parlement of Paris subsequently began legal proceedings against him, and he went to England, thus becoming perhaps the first *émigré*. It is ironic that a few years later he became a principal organizer of *émigré* resistance from Coblenz, working with the very men who had driven him from office and blackened his reputation.

The queen persuaded Louis to make Brienne principal minister. Hoping for a cardinal's hat, Brienne was not a religious man, but was reputed to be an enlightened one. However, he had no policy of his own to offer, and as the Notables were in no mood to compromise they were dismissed in May, though Lafayette took the opportunity of demanding a National Assembly. When the minister, surprisingly, appealed to the Parlement of Paris, it demanded the calling of the Estates General. In August two taxes had to be registered by a *lit de justice*, and when the Parlement declared this unconstitutional, it was exiled to Troyes.

Tempers were running high, but the financial situation had not improved and the diplomatic failure in the Dutch crisis emphasized the need for a quick settlement. Brienne recalled the Parlement, but well organized disputes continued, and in November Louis exiled the Duc d'Orléans to his estates by a *lettre de cachet*. Anticipating a royal attack, the Parlement in May 1788 published a declaration of the fundamental laws of the kingdom. To contemporaries, this sounded splendid revolutionary stuff – but it did not remove privilege; it was not the language to be heard the next year. However, the magistrates took a collective oath to serve in no assembly that might arbitrarily replace the Parlement – a procedure the Third Estate was to follow in the Tennis Court Oath of June 1789. Now the king showed his power, for he was not without resources. He arrested two leading magistrates and reduced the privileges of all the Parlements. They were not exiled, as Maupeou had required in 1771, but it was something in the nature of a royal *coup d'état*: however it was not followed up – and it had come too late, for there was already revolt in the provinces.

The magistrates were able to represent Louis as a reactionary delaying the calling of the Estates General. Demonstrations and serious disorder were widespread. In June the Church Assembly voted only 1,800,000 livres, instead of the 12 million some had hoped for, and protested against the suspension of the Parlement. There were riots in Toulouse and Dijon. At Pau in Béarn a band of mountaineers (precursors of the fleeing peasants of the Great Fear?) invaded the town, convinced that heavier taxes were to be levied. At Rennes in Brittany, the Parlement and Provincial Estates were behind some serious riots. The old bogey of a *pacte de famine* was raised against the king in many areas. In July the Dauphiné nobles illegally convoked the traditional Provincial Estate for the first time since 1628, and on the advice of Mounier and Barnave decided to double the representation of the Third Estate, to meet in common and to vote 'by head' – a decision foreshadowing 1789. Few were killed in this *révolte nobiliaire*, but it was clear that royal troops could not be relied upon, that government had broken down and that the monarchy was faced by that crisis that Louis XV had foreseen in his letter to the Duchesse de Choiseul – *'ils pourraient bien mettre sa couronne en danger'*.

Brienne surrendered and in August announced that the Estates General would be called for May 1789. A fortnight later he resigned, despite the efforts of the queen – for Louis, with some repugnance, was compelled to recall the popular Necker. A second Assembly of Notables was summoned to advise on the calling of the Estates, which had not met since 1614. On 23 September, at the height of their popularity as defenders of 'liberty', the Parlement made a triumphal re-entry into Paris, Brienne was burnt in effigy and the popular demonstrations degenerated into riots. The monarchy, whose original intention had been merely to secure reform to avert bankruptcy, had been defeated by its natural ally, the nobility; but the nobility was in fact, defending its privileges, and crowned its revolt by forcing an unwanted though popular minister on the king. In 1788, a chronicler would have noted the nobility's successful efforts to regain a commanding position in the state: no one foresaw the sweeping triumph of the bourgeoisie.

[7] THE APPEAL TO THE PEOPLE

On 25 September, the situation changed fundamentally. Until then the Parlements had posed as the champion of 'constitutionalism' against a despotic monarchy: they now declared in favour of convoking the Estates General according to the 1614 pattern. It was clear that a formidable coalition of privilege faced the Third Estate – for the Clergy had favoured the 1614 model too. The name of institutions matters less than their powers and the way in which they are organized: the 1614 procedure was for the three Estates, of about 300 members each, to meet separately and vote on every measure within their own assemblies 'by head', i.e. a simple majority; but then each Estate had one collective vote. In terms of 1789, the result would be obvious: the single votes of the two privileged bodies would defeat any measure to abolish privilege, though all 300 members of the Third Estate voted for it. The bourgeois were practical men: a 1614 Estates General was no use to them. This is why the Tennis Court Oath of the following June was so important – the crisis over procedure was fully developed in the previous September; it is another reason for dating the Revolution from the *révolte nobiliaire*. The popularity of the Parlement collapsed with their declaration and the struggle between king and aristocracy was transformed into one between privileged and unprivileged – 'War between the Third Estate and the other two Orders', as Mallet du Pan put it. Had the king at this juncture conceded double representation to the Third Estate (thus making them numerically equal to the other two combined) and vote 'by head' in a single assembly, instead of by separate Order, he would have saved the monarchy. Instead he allowed the former to be granted without credit to himself, and the latter was forced on him in circumstances that showed his cause was already lost. It is not, therefore, entirely true to say that to secure reform the king appealed to the Third Estate against the privileged Orders. With a show of simple courage, the bourgeoisie was to seize the initiative and to owe its victory to itself alone.

A certain amount of direction was given to bourgeois agitation in the winter of 1788-9 by the appearance of a 'Patriot Party', whose members were to play a vital rôle in the Revolution. It was composed of great liberal nobles and leading bourgeois and was dominated by a 'Committee of Thirty' – Talleyrand, Condorcet, Lafayette, Mirabeau, Sieyès (the latter two having contacts with Orléans) were prominent members. They had agents in the provinces and produced many pamphlets. But really everyone was waiting for Necker to decide how the Estates should meet. Personally he preferred the English model – the career open to talents and a House of Lords – but he was a weak man and had enemies at court. The current Assembly of Notables favoured the 1614 procedure and the Royal Princes warned the king solemnly of the threat to privilege and property rights implicit in the Third Estate demands. But the intendants reported threats of civil war and, on 27 December, Necker produced a 'Result' of Council, doubling the Third Estate but omitting any reference to voting procedure. The Third Estate declared this a victory: riots were frequent, and in Brittany a minor civil war between privileged and unprivileged broke out.

The elections produced some odd results. Since all the *curés* had the vote, no minor bishop was elected to the First Estate, and only a few major ones. Sens, Toul, even the archbishop of Lyons, Primate of all Gaul, failed to be elected. In all there were 42 bishops (including Talleyrand of Autun), 55 abbés, 7 monks and 205 *curés* – who were in effect to decide the fate of the Estates General. Brittany refused to send any representatives to the Second Estate, and the majority of those returned were impoverished provincial nobles determined to maintain their feudal rights; there were a few Court nobles, and perhaps 90 liberals – though only 47 were prepared to join the Third Estate at the beginning, and Lafayette was not one of them. With so few liberal nobles returned, there was little chance of copying the English revolution of 1688; in a sense, it was the provincial nobles' refusal to compromise that produced the Terror. The 610 members of the Third Estate were mostly lawyers – not one was a peasant and only one a working man. Sieyès and Mirabeau (a derogated noble) were already well known; Mounier and Barnave had made their names in Dauphiné; but most were prosperous honest folk with no clear policy though some had preconceived ideas. (A study of the membership of the Estates General is in Cobban's *The Myth of the French Revolution*, H. K. Lewis, 1955.) The progress of the Revolution was to throw up the great leaders to overcome crises of daunting height.

Each Estate was to draw up a *cahier de doléances*, and Malouet urged Necker to 'influence' them; but he declined and so lost a vital opportunity of directing bourgeois activity. The Committee of Thirty and the Duc d'Orléans circulated 'models' and there

were many 'models' of local origin – the Paris politicians did not
dictate the form of the local *cahiers*. There were three stages to
the drawing up of the *cahiers:* first, a local meeting, where the
bigger landowners tended to dominate, drew up a local one; these
were summarized into a *cahier* for the constituency, or bailiwick;
and ultimately a single *cahier* was produced for each Estate. It
was in consolidating the bailiwick *cahiers* that middle class
influence was most pronounced: even the local ones were drawn
up by the lawyer, clergy or wealthy peasant, for illiteracy was
widespread in rural France. The peasants' local social grievances
were frequently the ones left out at the editing stage – this is why
the *cahiers* must be treated with caution as evidence of popular
feeling in any real sense of the term.

In general, the Third Estate wanted to end feudal rights and
privileges (without infringing property rights) and to gain civil
equality. Some were anxious to secularize Church lands to solve
the financial crisis. The Clergy wanted to maintain the privilege of
their Order, and so did the Nobles, who were also anxious to stop
any bourgeois buying his way into the aristocracy – for quite
opposite reasons they agreed with the Third Estate that 'venality' should be abolished. Both Nobles and Clergy were prepared
to sacrifice their fiscal immunities only on the strictest of conditions that would have preserved those very inequalities that
the Third Estate sought to end. All agreed on the necessity of
destroying ministerial 'despotism' and securing individual
liberty (though these were phrases that were not clearly defined)
and control over taxation. There was much self-interest in the
cahiers – the commune of Morlaas (Béarn) 'demanded to know
why they should become Frenchmen rather than Béarnais', and
Navarre, regarding itself as a separate kingdom, refused to send
deputies. But in general they indicated an extensive desire for
reform, with little attention to practical details. Above all, they
demonstrated the great gap in intention and motive between the
privileged and unprivileged. Their production had heightened
political activity and given a significance to the Estates General
beyond that of an Assembly called to assist the crown in its
financial difficulties.

PART III
The Second Phase: 1789–92

[8] THE MONARCHY LOSES THE INITIATIVE

No one foresaw the vigour of the Revolution, despite the widespread feeling that a new era was about to begin, and despite the serious disturbances of 1788. Barentin, who was in charge of the ceremonial opening of the Estates General at Versailles on 5 May 1789, can be forgiven for seeking to keep the Third Estate deputies in their place: few of the privileged would have thought to treat them as equals! At any rate they were not obliged to listen to the king on their knees, as their predecessors of 1614 had done; but the arrangements were such as gratuitously to humiliate them. Yet there were many provincial bourgeois deputies who would have been only too happy to be told what to do – a little imagination in dealing with them, and a King's Party might have been formed from the outset among them. Instead, their inferior status was impressed upon them, and in the opening speeches they were given no leadership – the king made it clear he was not prepared to lose any of his power, and Necker's speech was so long, it had to be finished for him by an assistant. By the end of the opening session there was a hardening in the ranks of the Third Estate: not even Necker had proposed the reforms they desired. Their discontent provided fertile ground for rumours of an aristocratic plot to snatch the revolution from them.

Without clear leadership the Estates were left much to their own devices which meant that the Crown had lost the initiative.

For more than a month the Estates were bogged down in arid
procedural arguments which prevented any discussion of reform.
The arguments were complex and legalistic and were conducted
with the utmost care, for everyone knew that the king's reply to
revolutionary action could easily be to dissolve the Estates,
besides what further punishments he might reserve for 'trouble-
some' members. The arguments should not be passed over, for
they ended with a defeat for the monarchy from which it never
recovered. The dispute centred on the 'verification of powers' –
should the Estates meet separately or as a body to check
election returns and verify the powers of deputies? Following the
1614 procedure, the Nobles on 11 May constituted themselves a
separate Chamber – to meet in common would mean 'voting by
head' and the double representation of the Third Estate would
ensure a bourgeois majority. It was exactly for this reason that
the bourgeoisie wanted sessions to be in common, for otherwise
the vote of the Nobles' Estate would block any attempt to
abolish privilege. Everyone realized that behind the verification
of powers lay the *'réunion des ordres'*. Understandably, the
Third Estate refused to constitute itself a separate chamber, or
to transact business, and would not even elect a president.

Since the king did not intervene everything depended on the
First Estate, where there was a big majority of *curés* most of
whom would not object to joining the bourgeoisie, provided it
did not involve sacrificing clerical corporate organization. They
suggested conferences, but when these proved useless, Mirabeau
suggested inviting the clergy to join the Third Estate. Only by
skilful delaying tactics were the *curés* prevented from accepting
the invitation. Necker then suggested further conferences with
the royal ministers. These achieved nothing as they were thought
to be a government ruse to stop the *curés* joining. On 10 June,
Sieyès proposed the other Estates be invited to join the Third in
calling over a common roll of delegates: the roll was called
between 12 and 14 June, only a few *curés* and none of the nobles
– not even Lafayette – joining them. On 17 June the Third Estate,
after a violent debate, took the audacious step of calling themselves the National Assembly (changed to Constituent Assembly

on 9 July), an action which infringed the authority of the king himself. The deputies were well aware of the danger they were running, but they counted on support from Paris, from some liberal nobles, and from the *curés*. On 19 June the clergy voted to join the Third Estate. The *curés* had blunted the edge of privilege: if the king did not intervene, the aristocracy was lost.

Since 4 June the king had been in mourning at Marley for the death of the dauphin. There, surrounded by reactionary nobles led by his brother Artois, he resolved to act and on 19 June decided to hold a Royal Session to overawe the Third Estate, settle the procedural problems and propose reforms. But the Royal Session was delayed until the 23rd, because the queen objected to the reform programme. As early as May, Necker had drawn up a scheme curiously similar to the Charter granted by Louis XVIII in 1814: his proposals were rejected and, if he was not dismissed, he was at least absent from the Royal Session. It was, perhaps, the last moment when Necker could have gained control of events.

On 20 June the Third Estate found their hall closed and guarded by soldiers: realizing their danger, they adjourned to the nearby Tennis Court and there swore the famous Oath that Mounier proposed 'never to separate ... until the Constitution of the Kingdom shall be laid and established on secure foundations'. It was an action reminiscent of that of the Paris Parlement in the previous year (see page 44) and it bound the deputies together. On 22 June most of the clergy joined, so did the nobles of Dauphiné – the purpose of the Royal Session, fatally delayed, was already thwarted.

Four thousand troops had been concentrated round Versailles and more round Paris: clearly, the king had determined to assert his authority. It would be like the humbling of the Parlements in 1771. The Royal Session went well and the king's speech was a good one, in effect suggesting something like a constitutional monarchy, but siding with privilege, requiring the deputies to disperse and meet separately. The nobles withdrew and cheered the king and queen. When it was observed that the Third Estate and some clergy remained, they were ordered again to leave.

'The assembled nation cannot receive orders', replied Bailly, and their most effective spokesman, Mirabeau, said they would move only at bayonet point. Troops were sent to clear the hall, but it seems they were turned back by some liberal nobles, and the king did not persist in his demand. Eventually, on 27 June, he requested the nobles to join the new assembly. Thus the Third Estate had won a tremendous victory, and the bourgeois revolution follows naturally from it. However, on 26 June, troop concentrations round Paris and Versailles were increased. Necker might remain as a minister, but Barentin and the reactionaries dictated royal policy.

The popular picture of an indolent king petulantly accepting the '*réunion des ordres*' is not borne out by the careful military preparations in June and July; indeed the difficulty is to explain why such preparations met with so severe a defeat. The court was well aware of the danger of political riots – perhaps the royal surrender of 23 June was for fear of a repetition of the riots of the previous day, when a crowd had demonstrated against the rumour that Necker had been dismissed. The soldiers had refused to fire on the crowd – the court could not rely on their loyalty, hence the need to call foreign mercenary regiments to their aid. Arthur Young passed one marching to Paris on 9 July, and between 5 and 20 July some 18,000 troops were due to arrive – although shortage of food and the Treasury's lack of money hindered the movements. The intention was to dissolve the Assembly by force and replace Necker by Breteuil, who arrived at Versailles on 10 July. Next day Necker was dismissed and set off for Switzerland. It was then that Paris saved the Assembly and swept the Ancien Régime away.

The news of Necker's dismissal caused consternation in Paris on 12 July and there was a clash with the royal cavalry – Marat later boasted of having led a charge. Next day Danton was urging the people to arm themselves against the troops that surrounded them. On the 13th communications with Versailles were cut by soldiers closing the Sèvres and Saint-Cloud bridges; in the east of the city, Launay, governor of the Bastille, moved his cannon into the embrasures to cover the faubourg Saint-Antoine.

In self defence a committee of Electors who had chosen the
deputies to the Third Estate formed a National Guard and the
people clamoured for arms. Flesselles, the old provost, tempor-
ized, but arms were taken from the Arsenal, the Hôtel de Ville,
the Invalides and gun-shops (the gunsmith later claimed a total
of 115,118 livres compensation – vainly). There were not enough
arms and the cry went up that there were arms at the Bastille.
This was why the crowd marched to the Bastille on 14 July, not
to sack it, or release the seven prisoners it contained. But the
fortress was the symbol of royal power in the capital, and its
guns were menacing the homes of the crowd. That the fortress
fell – that it was even attacked – was due to Launay's incompe-
tence.

The Electors sent three officers to negotiate for arms and the
withdrawal of the cannon: Launay invited them to lunch. Time
passed and the crowd suspected treachery. Thuriot was sent in
to ask for the surrender of the fortress: half an hour after he
disappeared, the crowd lowered the drawbridge into the inner
courtyard and streamed in. Launay lost his head and gave the
order to fire. One defender was killed in the unequal struggle that
followed; of the crowd, 98 were killed and 73 wounded: when two
detachments of mutinous French Guards arrived and trained
three cannon on the main gate, Launay surrendered on promise
of safe conduct. It is amazing that the crowd did not exact a
terrible vengence: after days of tension, they supposed that they
had been invited into the inner courtyard merely to be shot down:
yet only three officers and three men were murdered and
Launay was escorted to the Hôtel de Ville, but there was murdered. So was Flesselles, who had 'witheld' arms from the people.
Their heads were paraded on pikes.

The men who took the Bastille were mostly small traders and
artisans, not vagabonds in the pay of the Duc d'Orléans. Its
capture meant the loss of the capital to the monarchy: it meant
more than this – it meant that the royal coup was now called off,
that the people of Paris had saved the Revolution. Abroad it was
welcomed as the triumph of political liberty over despotism –
for the cause of the Revolution was still popular in other count-

tries. In the course of the next few years, the Bastille was systematically demolished (it provided useful employment) and
Palloy, the builder who gained the demolition contract, made a
fortune out of the business.

The king was hunting when the Bastille was being stormed.
On his return, he found his plans ruined and contemplated
flight: two years later he admitted to Count Fersen that he had
missed his chance when he decided not to flee. And so he kept
his crown by implicitly recognizing a power in France superior
to himself – this was the real end of the Bourbon monarchy as it
had been understood up to that time. Bailly was elected Mayor
of Paris and Lafayette became first commander of the National
Guard – it was Lafayette who gave France the tricolour, the
symbolic synthesis of the old and the new France. On 17 July
the king came to Paris and accepted the tricolour: he was joy-
fully received, for people thought that he, like the Revolution,
had been saved from an aristocratic plot – there was still time
to save the monarchy as an institution. On 18 July he dismissed
Breteuil and recalled Necker: Louis's humiliation was complete –
but like the Bourbons of the Restoration, he learnt nothing from
it.

The failure of the royal coup was followed by a virtual breakdown of civil administration and public order. Many aristocrats,
like Artois, Condé, the Polignacs and Breteuil, fled. There were
widespread rumours of preparation for civil war and foreign
invasion. In Paris, Bertier de Sauvigny, the intendant, and his
father-in-law, Foullon de Doué (thought to have been in league
with Breteuil) were lynched on 22 July – 'Is this blood so pure
that one should regret to spill it?' asked Barnave, from the floor
of the National Assembly. In the provinces, Mme Roland agreed
with him: both were haunted by the fear of the aristocratic plot,
to destroy which, bloodshed was admissible.

The fear of an aristocratic plot to overthrow the Revolution
by force – perhaps bringing in foreign troops to do it – is one of
the keys to understanding the history of the Revolution. Ideas
of this nature were no doubt put about by the radical agitators
of the Palais Royal, but it seems that as early as May suspicions

of such a plot were already current in many parts of France, with
no artificial pressure to encourage them. The action of the court
in June and July merely added credence to the suspicions,
and the spontaneous action of Paris underlined the determination of France to have its Revolution. An aristocratic appeal for
foreign help had been precisely what the counter-revolutionaries
of Holland had made in 1788: it did not need a host of agitators
to get the people to rise and protect their Revolution against
the enemy from within. Almost the whole Third Estate believed
in the plot: in 1789 it was foiled and therefore the vigilance required to protect the Revolution died down. Three years later
the plot was clearly apparent with precisely those features that
had been ascribed to it in 1789. The September Massacres (1792)
and the Terror of 1793-4 fit naturally into the progress of the
Revolution: they were the logical conclusion to the taking of
the Bastille.

July 1789 saw a spontaneous municipal revolution – in some
towns local risings took place before 14 July. In Paris itself, the
Electors, who had chosen the Paris delegates of the Third
Estate, organized a municipal council (or commune) at the
Hôtel de Ville at the end of June; and all over France small
groups of resolute men overturned the closed corporations that
held power in the towns. Newly formed National Guards all over
the country took possession of local citadels and armed themselves against any aristocratic counter-revolution. The National
Guards took upon themselves the responsibility of maintaining
public order – many of them, in Barnave's phrase, were 'good
bourgeoisie'. It was they who restored order among the peasantry
for the majority of intendants abandoned their posts in July,
thus depriving the king of direct authority in the provinces.

Order had to be restored among the peasantry because the
disturbances of the spring (see page 33) had developed into a
peasants' revolt by the summer. Many factors contributed to
this – the bad harvest of 1788 and the resulting food shortage;
the disturbed political situation over the previous two years; the
sudden expectation of great changes arising from the calling of
the Estates General and the compilation of the *cahiers;* the fear

of an 'aristocratic plot' and the failure of the Estates General to meet the peasants' demands. There were, of course, sound political reasons why no progress had been made on legislative matters; furthermore, though willing to end feudal privilege, the lawyer deputies of the Third Estate were naturally anxious not to infringe property rights by hasty changes in feudal law. But such legal niceties meant little to hungry peasants – nor could it have escaped their notice that many bourgeois deputies were farming feudal dues and so would be unlikely to hasten the end of so profitable an investment.

Cambrésis and Picardy were aflame in May, and round Paris and Versailles peasants systematically exterminated game. There was no need for them to await events in the towns, but certainly 14 July had an electrifying effect throughout France. In Normandy, Franche-Compté, Alsace and the Mâconnais there were risings: soon there was widespread disorder which, between 20 July and 6 August, became an amazing demonstration of mass hysteria, called *la Grande Peur*. It began with rumours of vagabonds and brigands, even of foreign troops, advancing towards villages: people fled in terror as the rumours spread – sometimes over vast distances. Nantes and Beauvais, Champaigne, Maine, Angoulême and the Mâconnais were particularly affected and in Dauphiné there was a full-scale revolt. Although the disturbances were spontaneous and unorganized there was remarkable similarity in what occurred all over France – evidence of the solidarity of peasant feeling. For all the hysteria, violence to the person was rare and only a few châteaux were burnt down. The peasants' chief purpose seems to have been to destroy the *terriers*, the records of feudal dues; in addition, enclosures were torn down, innovations removed and commons and forests re-occupied. The peasant was ensuring that the agricultural revolution should not occur in France.

Faced with such a threat to civil authority and the fear that it would become a real *jacquerie*, the middle-class National Guards wherever possible did much to restore order – to have used royal troops, even supposing them to have been reliable, would have been too dangerous, for they might then have been used against the Assembly. In the Mâconnais over a hundred peasants were hanged. But what really saved the day was the famous night of 4 August, when many feudal rights and fiscal immunities were surrendered – not in a spontaneous burst of generosity (they had had at least since May for that!) but as an instrument of public control to stop the disturbances.

A manoeuvre to induce the voluntary surrender of certain feudal rights with the support of the great liberal nobles, had been planned by the radical 'cave' of the Breton Club (subsequently to become the Jacobin Club, but too much should not be made of this). The Duc d'Aiguillon was chosen to move the motion, but he was anticipated by Lafayette's brother-in-law, the Vicomte de Noailles (being a younger son he did not own the family estate and so was nick-named Jean Sansterre; but he was wealthy as a result of all the pensions he had received at court). As the debate proceded, things got out of hand, for in a wave of enthusiasm feudal rights and taxation privileges, venality and even municipal and provincial privileges were declared abolished. The Assembly recovered itself a few days later, distinguishing between feudal and 'real' rights, the latter to be redeemable – the *cens* was to be redeemed at a very high rate indeed. Even the tithe, suppressed without indemnity, was to be continued until an act on public worship was passed. Many peasants, however, refused to pay any further dues or redemption fees. Feudalism, in fact, in some forms survived 4 August. Peasants had to wait until after the rising of 10 August 1792 before payments for which a specific title deed could not be produced (how many had perished in the Great Fear!) were officially abolished without compensation; and it was not until after the Jacobin *coup d'état* of 2 June 1793 that all remaining feudal obligations were abolished.

The peasants had taken the initiative; the burning of the *terriers* had forced the Assembly's hand – it also impelled it towards the Declaration of Rights. The feudal framework of society might have survived a little while longer without their action: it was not the writings of the *philosophes*, nor the actions of political leaders that secured the social revolution of 4 August

1789, but the mass action of unknown peasants. They had gained their prime objective: the radical and dynamic social changes that resulted from it interested them less than their relief from increasing feudal dues and the threat of further enclosure by landlords defended by courts and Parlements alike. The peasants do not now leave the Revolution, for it is they who defend it in the darkest days of 1792-4, and they who send their sons to the armies of Napoleon: they continue their own course, tacitly supporting a Revolution that gave them freedom and land but no longer act as so powerful an independent force upon its progress. As Napoleon recognized, they remained the backbone of France.

4 August cleared the ground for a constitution. The Declaration of the Rights of Man and of the Citizen (Lafayette had submitted proposals for this as early as 11 July) sought to create a unity among Frenchmen that the monarchy had always failed to provide. It was no vague compilation of good intentions (see page 16) but the foundation of the Constitution and a means of legalizing the revolutionary action that had so far been taken. It was a declaration of universal application, based on the revolutionary concept that sovereignty was vested in the people. The delegates themselves admitted that the Rights were essentially relative, and that they could not be the same in war as in peace.

If Louis XVI had capitulated to violence, he was still prepared to offer resistance to the Assembly. On 5 August he wrote to the Archbishop of Arles to say that he could not sanction the reforms of 4 August, and he maintained his refusal despite the procedure for redemption, so favourable to the aristocracy. Nor was he prepared to sign the Declaration of Rights. So strong was the traditional feeling for the monarchy that the deputies were not immediately prepared to take action: instead they debated whether the king should have an absolute, or a suspensive veto, or none at all. There were frequent negotiations, many of the 'Patriot' party, fearing the recurrence of popular violence, wished to compromise – a suspensive veto for the king's acceptance of the August decrees. When the suspensive veto was agreed to on 11 September, and the king still had not given his consent to the decrees, however, many delegates felt they had been cheated.

In Paris neither Bailly nor Lafayette was fully in control; there was much pamphleterring – Marat began his '*L'Ami du Peuple*', promoting the cause of the poor, in September. An attempt to march on Versailles to bring back the king on 30 August was foiled, but there was great popular excitement over the veto, which was regarded as a further symbol of the aristocratic plot. Rumour was as widespread as ever suspecting aristocrats of counter-revolution – with good cause, for the Marquis de Favras, leader of a group called 'French Regeneration', was laying plans for the king's flight – and Mounier, fearing further disorder, was secretly urging the king to adjourn the Assembly to Soissons. Louis rejected both plans. There were already signs of a further royalist coup. On 14 September he summoned the Flanders regiment – which he hoped would prove more reliable than the French Guards. They arrived with great pomp on 23 September, and Paris was as disturbed as in July. Talk of a march on Versailles was common, and the National Guard provided an armed nucleus. It seems that the 'October Days' were deliberately planned as a political demonstration to coerce the king; the Duc d'Orléans probably supplied funds, and Mirabeau and possibly Lafayette, were implicated. But it was economic pressures that actually touched off the March of the Women.

The Revolution had increased unemployment, especially in the luxury trades, as a result of the emigration – some 200,000 passports were issued in two months. Money was scarce – much was being transferred to Holland and England. Many servants were dismissed, and there was a serious drop in money available to private charities. Bread was scarce and costly: the harvest had been good, but peasants stayed away from markets fearing disorder, and the mills of Paris could not grind enough flour because of the lack of wind and the low level of the water. Queues formed at baker's shops, and guards were necessary: there was a return of fears of a 'famine plot'. It was easy to promote the idea of marching on Versailles to save the king from the aristocratic plot and to bring both him and food back to Paris.

Royalist imprudence provoked the actual outbreak: at a banquet for the officers of the Flanders regiment on 2 October, the royal family was cheered and the tricolour insulted. Large crowds in the Palais Royal, many of them women who were especially intemperate in their references to the queen, gathered on the 3rd. A demonstration planned for next day was checked by the National Guard, but Lafayette took no precautions on 5 October when a crowd of women, not all of them *sans-culottes*, pillaged the Hôtel de Ville, and putting Maillard, a veteran of the Bastille, at their head, set off in the rain for Versailles. The National Guard petitioned Lafayette to go too in order to avenge the insult to the tricolour: 'The king is fooling us all, you included', cried a guardsman. On his white horse, Lafayette harangued the crowd, but at last the Commune sent him off at 4 p.m. to 'invite' the king to return to Paris.

The king was out hunting again. He returned at 3 p.m. and the council advised the use of force to stop the women, and urged the king to flee to Rambouillet. Whilst Louis was consulting the queen, the women arrived. Promised bread, many withdrew. The crisis was over, nothing of a political nature having been gained. But when Lafayette arrived at 9 p.m., the council insisted on flight, the queen and Mounier agreeing. Louis, however, refused to become a fugitive and provoke civil war: instead, he accepted the August decrees – so much had been gained – but gave no answer to the request to come to Paris. In the early morning several hundred demonstrators entered the palace through an unguarded gateway, and after some bloodshed penetrated to the queen's apartments; she escaped, half dressed, to the king, saving her life and honour. An ugly situation was only relieved when Lafayette appeared on the balcony with the royal family and the king yielded to cries of 'To Paris!' A long procession of carriages, containing 'the baker, the baker's wife and the baker's boy', guarded by Lafayette, together with a delegation from the Assembly, and a supply of bread, returned to Paris.

The king, now in Paris, was not yet a prisoner of the capital, but the monarchists had lost the day. No one paid much attention to the flood of *émigrés*, nor was there any alarm at the break-up of the 'Patriot' party – the moderates were overthrown and went into opposition. Mounier retired to Dauphiné to become perhaps the first federalist (compare page 127), and soon, since his attempt to rouse counter-revolution failed, he, too, became an *émigré*. The king was still popular and the fiction that he agreed with the Assembly was maintained: safe in Paris he was no longer in danger of being implicated in the 'aristocratic plot'. The *sans-culottes* had staked their claim to be considered: they could now be excluded from political influence only with the greatest difficulty. The peasants had overthrown feudalism, but deputies were determined that the *sans-culottes* should not over-throw the political power of the bourgeoisie. Having no more immediate need for their assistance, the Assembly, on 21 October (two days after it had come to Paris following the king – it was in no hurry to come), introduced severe measures to curb disturbances and pamphleteering. At the same time, however, both Commune and Assembly took energetic measures to solve the food crisis and so a period of relative calm, culminating, perhaps, in the great Feast of Federation, on 14 July 1790, slowly developed in the capital. But the deputies should not be credited with too much foresight: it is, no doubt, going too far to argue, as some left-wing historians do, that with an eye to the main chance they utilized the motive power of the *sans-culottes* to promote bourgeois ends, while disregarding as far as they could the aims of their allies. The political crises of the Revolution are too complex in their nature to be explicable merely in terms of the class struggle.

The events of 1789 had resulted in a completely changed distribution of political power: the Revolution seemed on the way to producing great and durable reforms. It was not the fault of the deputies that their efforts were to lead to twenty years of war.

[9] THE WORK OF THE CONSTITUENT ASSEMBLY

The Estates General had been summoned to deal with the financial crisis: the Third Estate intended to give France a Constitution. They were in no hurry to complete either task, lest they should lose their opportunity of passing all their reforms. Indeed, some of the important provisions of the Constitution arose out of the political difficulties that occurred after July 1789. Furthermore, the Assembly was not alone in forming public opinion: the peasants continued to follow their own course; royalists began marshalling the forces of counter-revolution; and in Paris the Assembly had many rivals. Its galleries were filled with the general public – fashionable folk; it was not until after the flight to Varennes that the *sans-culottes* predominated. Following Mirabeau's example, Lafayette and other leading politicians paid supporters to dominate the galleries. The cafés continued to be centres of discussion; the stage, too, was very politically conscious; pamphlets and journals proliferated; but the most important centres were the clubs that came to dominate the progress of the Revolution.

At Versailles, the Breton delegates had been well organized: on moving to Paris, they formed the Society of the Friends of the Constitution, in November 1789, which met in the old Jacobin convent near the Assembly, and so was called the Jacobin Club. It was open to non-delegates but charged a high subscription and was therefore largely bourgeois, although it numbered over a thousand by December 1790. Its views were well known through its official journal and, from October 1791, it held its debates in public. Affiliated Jacobin Clubs sprang up in provincial towns maintaining close contact with the Paris Club by correspondence and delegations; in this way it wielded considerable authority throughout the country. The system seems merely to have grown up, but it has been copied by many revolutionary organizations, even in our own day. Many politicians found it best to be members, even though the club was generally 'left wing', and it was through the Jacobins, that Robespierre was able to maintain his political influence during the period of the Legislative Assembly.

The Society of the Rights of Man, called the Cordeliers after its early meeting place, was less a debating club than an 'action committee' of the *sans-culottes*. It charged a low subscription and was more violent than the Jacobins: Danton first established his authority through the Club. In 1790 many Popular and Fraternal Societies sprang up patronized by the Cordeliers and often influenced by Marat. Not to be outdone, the royalists had their clubs and the moderates had, for example, Malouet's *Impartiaux* and Lafayette's *Club de '89*. Provincial towns had their clubs too; the Friends of the Constitution (Jacobin) Club at Bordeaux proved a training ground for some of the Girondin deputies of the Legislative Assembly and the Convention.

The Assembly's constructive work ranged over a wide field and in many cases proved to be of lasting value and importance. The Declaration of Rights established a set of principles that released a great fund of energy and helped to found a new, durable society. No doubt the deputies had their heads full of the ideas of the *philosophes*, yet their reforms were the reforms of practical men. Their transformation of the judiciary, beginning on 4 August, when seigneurial jurisdiction was renounced, gave France a unified legal system for the first time. Justices and judges were elected, but proved so independent that they had to be purged during the Terror. The jury was introduced (though confined, despite Robespierre's protests, to 'active' citizens); many old punishments and public tortures disappeared, the guillotine was merciful although it performed in public, but Robespierre failed to secure the abolition of the death sentence. Napoleon was to systematize these and other reforms: he was the residuary legatee of the Revolution.

In local government order was brought out of the chaos of conflicting divisions that typified the Ancien Régime. France was divided into eighty-three Departments, each subdivided into districts, cantons and communes. As a result, the ancient provinces were merged with France and local provincialism weakened. The royal office of intendant was abolished, but central authority continued to be exercised through the elected local '*procureur général syndic*'. A great deal of decentralization was achieved, but the Jacobins, under stress of war, had to resort to centralization in 1793. In June 1790 Paris was redivided into forty-eight Sections each with about 12,500 people, with the city's armed guard controlled by the Commune. These Sections were to be vitally important in the crises of the next few years: the tocsin rung in any of them might herald the overthrow of a government and more work for the guillotine.

The 1791 Constitution proved to be so limited a monarchy as to be in effect a Republic. The crises of 1789 had already given the deputies cause to distrust Louis XVI and in October of that year he had become 'King of the French', a change of name of infinite significance with its implicit assertion of national sovereignty. His veto, which both Robespierre and Barnave had questioned, was suspensive for two legislatures (four years); he could choose ministers, but they could not be members of the Assembly; ministers had to countersign his own orders, and he could not initiate legislation. He was allowed a civil list and was to be more of a civil servant than a king. The issue was underlined in the great debate on the right to declare peace or war. In 1790 a dispute over the possession of Nootka Sound (Vancouver, British Columbia) had broken out between Britain and Spain. Spain appealed to France for aid under the Family Compact: the Assembly refused aid. The Jacobins feared a war would increase royal power and demanded the revision of all alliances in the name of the people. Lafayette, Mirabeau and the moderates wanted diplomacy to remain in the king's hands. After violent pamphleteering a compromise was agreed allowing the king to declare war or make peace, after the Assembly had given its decision.

The dispute ended with the passing of the famous declaration renouncing in the name of the French people any war of conquest. The wars that followed seemed to nullify this declaration; but the Jacobins were looking to the past, not the future; they were saying that diplomacy and war had ceased to be the sport of kings.

The Constitution provided for the election of a single-chamber Legislature elected for two years independent of the king. In place of privilege of birth, was put privilege of wealth – Robespierre and Marat might denounce a new 'aristocracy of wealth' but the country was not much moved. The 'passive' citizens – domestic servants and the poor – lacked a stake in the community and, oddly enough, were feared as docile tools of counter-revolutionaries. The 'active' citizens, some 4¼ million out of 26 million, had a vote if they paid in direct taxation the equivalent of three days' wages of a labourer. Clearly it was to be a bourgeois 'republic'. Election was to be indirect, active citizens voting for 'electors', who qualified by paying the equivalent of ten days' wages. Deputies had to possess land worth £60 a year and to be paying the equivalent of fifty days' wages (the famous '*marc d'argent*', which was modified after the flight to Varennes – see page 77). Only 'active' citizens could enrol in the National guard. A procedure was also adopted that would have meant that any change in the Constitution would take ten years to become effective. All this was less a denial of political rights to the majority, than a declaration of political realism – England did not have manhood suffrage before 1885. The deputies were not reorganizing France on the basis of simple abstract principles. Even Robespierre's famous 'self-denying ordinance' of 16 May 1791, which disallowed deputies of the Constituent Assembly from sitting in the succeeding Legislative Assembly, was followed by the law of 28 May which, in effect, provided these same deputies with the chance of well-paid jobs in Department administration. Perhaps the *Loi le Chapelier* (le Chapelier was an original member of the Breton Club and had presided in the Assembly on the famous night of the 4 August) of 14 June 1791 did savour somewhat of *physiocrat* principles, since, in the name of freedom of contract, it forbade combinations of employers and employees alike. But the deputies were fearful of disorder among the Paris workers, and the law was directed primarily against them. It outlawed trade unions and the right to strike – but it was not formally abrogated until 1884. Certainly there was no Trade Disputes Act of 1789.

The deputies were similarly practical in dealing with the financial chaos. Many held *physiocrat* views and regarded any economic controls as bad: yet existing controls were not suddenly swept away. In due course they were to be forced, much against their will, to impose a control on commodity prices in the crisis of 1793 (see page 134). Necker, understandably, had no solution to the impossible financial position of 1789. The nationalization of church property, if a violent expedient, seemed the obvious answer – Calonne and some *cahiers* had advocated it, and estimates of the value of church property, often absurdly exaggerated, encouraged the view that here lay the answer to the problem. On 10 October 1789 Talleyrand proposed the nationalization of church property and in December a new department of State was established to sell church lands and to issue Treasury bills of exchange (*assignats*) on the basis of the proceeds of sale. The *assignats* were unpopular and people hoarded coinage – the failure of John Law's scheme, seventy years before, had destroyed faith in paper money. But the *assignats* were made legal tender on 17 April 1790 – they were a political weapon as well as a financial expedient, for they represented the sale of church property and they bound to the Revolution all who purchased. Originally they were intended merely to extinguish the debt, but they proved an easy way of 'printing money' based on rosy calculations of the value of church property – long before the war aggravated the situation, their value was undermined, for some 2,500 million were issued in the first sixteen months of their existence. Necker, having completely lost control, was replaced (perhaps because of Mirabeau's intrigues) in September 1790. Inflation did not deter the Assembly, even though large numbers of counterfeit notes were in circulation within the first year. But the *assignats* saved the Revolution and paid for the beginning of the war; if their value declined to ridiculous proportions, it was not solely due to bad financial policy – the collapse of a currency is not unknown even in our own day.

The sales raised little opposition, although in some areas there were attempts at interference by clergy and nobles. Arrangements to help the small buyer had been made but, as the land was sold in blocks, the peasant bought perhaps only a sixth of the total, most going to bourgeois speculators. An opportunity to satisfy peasant land hunger had been lost and counter-revolutionaries exploited the consequent feeling of discontent. But religious troubles did not arise out of the sale of church lands – they came with the Civil Constitution of the Clergy.

The problem of reconciling the Roman Catholic Church with civil authority has always proved difficult, but the deputies were quite unprepared for the clerical reaction to their plans. They hoped to reform the church and bring it under state control while still recognizing the Pope's primacy over the church. Organizational reforms, including the redistribution of bishoprics to coincide with the eighty-three Departments, had not provoked any serious division among the clergy. Catherine the Great of Russia and Joseph II of Austria had carried out radical ecclesiastical changes without causing a papal condemnation and the deputies hoped for similar treatment – this was, perhaps, a little naïve, as the Civil Constitution of the Clergy, voted on 12 July 1790, made the church in effect a department of state with election of bishops and clergy, like any other public officer, by the active citizens. The king accepted it with grave misgivings, for he was a devout man. No one was quite prepared for the clerical opposition – hitherto parish priests had been revolutionaries, and had profited by it – their stipends had almost doubled. But the sacrifice of traditional corporate church government was too much for many priests.

The Pope kept silence until the following March; but long before then a Church Party had arisen. From the outset the politics of counter-revolution complicated the church question and the local disturbances and long uncertainty caused the Assembly, under pressure from the administration, to force the issue by insisting that every priest take an oath of loyalty to the Civil Constitution (27 November 1790). The king was in great distress but his reluctant agreement was extracted on 26 December. Seven bishops and about half the clergy took the oath –

there were great regional variations, but most of the clergy in West France refused and became 'non-jurors'. A religious war, in effect, had begun and the non-jurors became in many cases the spearhead of counter-revolution, which, for the first time, became an effective opposing force. Violent anticlericalism grew in proportion to the activities of the non-jurors.

The schism, threatening for a year, was openly declared when the Pope broke silence in March and April 1791, by denouncing the Revolution, the Declaration of Rights and the Civil Constitution. The possible loss of Avignon to France (annexed after a plebiscite in September 1791), the propaganda of *émigrés* and other Catholic powers, especially Spain, and the attitude of French cardinals in Rome all helped him to his decision. The deputies had raised a hornets' nest about them – unwittingly. The dangerously counter-revolutionary areas within France were all areas in which the non-jurors were strong. The schism lasted until Napoleon signed a new Concordat with the Pope in 1801.

During 1790 the most important man in France was the Marquis de Lafayette, one of the heroes of the American Revolution who had cast himself as the Washington of the French Revolution. Since the time of the Assembly of Notables his complacent hope had been to reconcile the opposing forces of the Revolution by promoting the cause of a limited monarchy supported by the wealthy propertied classes. From July 1789 he was commander of the National Guard and to a great extent public order depended on his personal moral authority. He had probably saved the monarchy in the October Days, and, in effect, the king was his prisoner. Yet, though anxious to preserve royal authority, he could never gain Louis's respect and the queen despised him. The tragedy was that he thought the king trusted him, when Louis was seeking a way to overthrow the Revolution.

Lafayette was a prig; and when Mirabeau, who at least understood politics, offered him his services, they were rebuffed by a man who liked his own position of pre-eminence and disliked Mirabeau's morals. Lafayette's popularity was immense, as was shown at the Feast of Federation on 14 July 1790, when patriots from all over France demonstrated the unity of France on the

Champ de Mars. Every suspected counter-revolutionary plot made his position as 'mayor of the palace' more secure. But his popularity began to wane in the Autumn of 1790 when military discipline began to disintegrate and a series of mutinies occurred. He suppressed them vigorously: some mutineers were hanged, others sent to the galleys: at Nancy Bouillé fought a pitched battle to defeat them. Lafayette's popularity declined until, by the spring of 1791, the 'hero of two worlds', galloping to and fro on his white charger, had become something of a figure of fun.

In 1791, seeking to arrest the course of the Revolution, he tried to form an alliance with the 'triumvirate', Dupont, Lameth and Barnave, and their supporters, who were anxious for a 'conservative' constitutional monarchy. But Robespierre ruined half their plans by promoting the law of 16 May, excluding deputies from the next Assembly – it was less a 'self-denying ordinance', indeed, than a defence of the Revolution. The other half was ruined by the king who ended any real hope for a constitutional monarchy by the flight to Varennes. When, shortly afterwards, Lafayette let the National Guard shoot on the poor petitioners of the Champ de Mars (see page 77), the action seemed not out of character. There were few regrets when he retired to his estates in September. A year later (August 1792), having failed to save the monarchy, he deserted to the enemies of France.

In the spring of 1791 the ideal of a limited monarchy was crumbling because of the actions of the monarch himself, and of clerical and aristocratic resistance. The unity of the Third Estate had not been maintained – indeed, the rift between rich and poor, enshrined in the Constitution's distinction between active and passive citizens, lay at the root of much of the violence of the Revolution. As yet, it showed itself in isolated incidents only; but it was to play its part in the Terror.

[10] THE FAILURE OF THE ROYAL COUNTER-REVOLUTION

Had he not died at the most propitious moment of his chequered career, the Comte de Mirabeau would have been one of the first victims of the Terror. Among the leaders of the early years of the Revolution were men like Necker and Lafayette who faded from the scene, and men like Robespierre and Danton who were to prove themselves worthy leaders in the nation's darkest hours; yet Mirabeau stands above them all as a leader of titanic energy with claims to statesmanship that have been championed by many historians. Mirabeau tried to save the monarchy; his failure is to be found in many reasons, not least in Louis XVI himself.

Strong, virile, thickset, with a pock-marked, ugly face, Mirabeau was a Wilkes-like figure – as profligate and as able, but with greater perseverance. He was much travelled, but his reputation excluded him from even Paris society. His own Order refused him as a delegate, so he sat for the Third Estate as a derogated noble. In the Assembly his predominance was assured from the beginning by his powers of leadership and grasp of politics yet, despite his services in June and July, the delegates trusted him so little and feared his ambition so much that the decree of 7 November 1789, preventing the king choosing his ministers in the Assembly, was passed largely to prevent Mirabeau becoming a ministerial dictator. It was a measure of his influence. A brilliant orator, he delivered his set speeches (many having been written for him) with a conviction all his own. He seems to have been the first to pack the public galleries with supporters and he was always active in the journalistic field. With little awareness of the feeling of the *sans-culottes*, he was always playing for popular support – J. M. Thompson, has called his death 'The first great death bed of the New Paganism'. In a modern world of mass electorates he would have been at home perhaps as a fascist leader, for his principal concern was to create a dominant executive capable of overriding all opposition. Hence his wish to establish a strong constitutional monarchy; *'administrer c'est gouverner; gourverner c'est regner'* was his motto.

From the outset his policy was clear – in December 1788 he wrote to Montmorin, the Foreign Minister, urging his plan for a strong monarchy. This is the dominant theme of his later correspondence with the court. Necker he disliked, and he gradually assumed much of the leadership Necker failed to give. Excluded from direct power by the 7 November decree, he endeavoured to achieve power through Lafayette, who had already offered him 50,000 livres to pay his debts and an ambassadorship at Constantinople (he refused the latter only). But both distrusted the other too much – 'Cromwell Grandison' said Mirabeau of Lafayette, and Lafayette knew Mirabeau would do most things for money. Ever resourceful, in May 1790 Mirabeau offered his services to the court through the intermediary of the Comte de La Marck, though he knew the queen detested him. The price was high: 200,000 livres to pay his debts, 6,000 a month and the promise of a million on the dissolution of the Assembly – but it was worth it to have Mirabeau on the side of the king. For Mirabeau was a dangerous man: his political chicanery, suspected at the time, is obvious from surviving correspondence. At the very time he was writing to Lafayette urging him to 'be a Richelieu, dominating the court in the interests of the Nation' (with Mirabeau as Father Joseph), he was indicating ways of destroying Lafayette's credit in the first of fifty Notes he wrote to the court through his friend La Marck. And all the while he was posing as the great champion of the people.

After the October Days, Mirabeau had written to the Comte de Provence urging him to get the king away from Paris where he was neither free nor safe. He suggested Rouen – away from the frontiers so as not to give rise to fears of an appeal to foreign troops – and, once free, to appeal to the Nation. Provence rejected the scheme as being sure to lead to civil war. But it was in essence this scheme that he proceeded to press on the court in his Notes the following year – regain the initiative, revise the Constitution, lead a strong executive. By August 1790 a touch of hysteria enters the Notes and, quite unabashed, he begins to advocate a policy of '*le pire*' – defeat the Revolution by promoting civil war and forcing a conflict over religion, discredit the Assembly and dismiss it after escaping from Paris, call a new royalist assembly (controlling the elections). The climax comes in the famous forty-seventh Note in which this policy is worked out at length in detail. His policy had become one of provoking a cataclysm in order to make the Revolution into a mouse; of playing at palace revolutions on a national scale with the happiness of twenty-six million people as the stakes. Certainly he had a plan, but whether it could work with a monarch like Louis XVI, or work at all, remains an open question. As La Marck said, Mirabeau was more monarchist than the monarch. He needed a Napoleon: but Napoleon had no need of a Mirabeau. Fortunately for himself, he died on 2 April 1791. Few suspected that for a year he had been in the pay of the court: he was given a hero's funeral and was the first to lie in the nation's Pantheon. When evidence of his venality with the court was published, his body was dragged out, to be replaced by that of a different friend of the people – Marat.

His death was fortunate also in that it came before the flight to Varennes which destroyed the monarchy this statesman *manqué* sought to save. The court might buy advice from Mirabeau; it did not intend to profit by it. Varennes would have destroyed his reputation and hopes as it did those of Lafayette and the moderates. It seemed that no one could save the monarchy from itself.

In 1788 the monarchy appeared to be appealing to the people against privilege: the crises of 1789 showed it had returned to reaction. Definite plans for the king's flight had been made then; more elaborate ones were made in 1790 and 1791. *Émigrés* abroad and reactionary nobles at home were promoting counter-revolution and both joined the court in appealing directly for foreign military aid to defeat the Revolution – in effect, Mirabeau's Notes were irrelevant.

In November 1789 Louis wrote secretly to Charles IV of Spain repudiating the public concessions wrung from him and seeking money and aid for counter-revolution. Similar messages were sent during the next three years – Mirabeau, Lafayette and the rest were building on a quicksand. Various plans for the king's flight, a rising of nobles and an invasion from Savoy culminated in Favras's plot in which both Mirabeau and Provence were implicated. Favras was discovered and executed in February 1790, without revealing his accomplices. To calm things, the king read a statement to the Assembly on 4 February 1790, declaring he accepted the new order of things unreservedly. It was one of a long series of deceptions: Louis XVI was no innocent.

Abroad, Artois was busy soliciting foreign aid from any willing source. In France royalists were equally busy with plots, some-times in collusion with Artois, like the one to foment civil war in the Midi. From June to October 1790 the royal family were at Saint-Cloud (they were not yet properly prisoners of Paris), and royalists made extensive plans for their escape – especially the 'Blacks', a well established group who were planning a march on Lyons to seize the town. Louis rejected their plans. He preferred restoration at the hands of a victorious 'enemy' prince, like the Emperor, to reinstatement at the hands of the privileged who would then be in a position to impose their will on the monarch. However, plans were well advanced for a rising in the south helped by an invasion of Sardinian troops under Artois. A police swoop killed the plan in December 1790, and the Auvergne nobles who were implicated, recalling Favras's fate, wisely emi-grated.

Louis's own plans for escape began actively in October 1790. In the previous June he had discovered that the Emperor Leopold of Austria was too cautious a man to intervene. Furthermore, Leopold, quite apart from having difficulties enough of his own, considered the changes being promoted by the Revolution were too similar to those he was himself sponsoring in his own domin-ions to warrant repression. In October Louis gave full powers to take charge of a secret project to ruin the Revolution, and to accredit royal agents to foreign courts, to Breteuil, the man who had replaced Necker in the abortive coup of July 1789, and who was now an *émigré*. The broad outline of royal plans for flight were clear: Bouillé, the suppressor of the Nancy mutiny, would

use his troops to defend the king, who would escape to the frontier, perhaps to Metz. The surprising thing is that the plans took
so long maturing. In December 1790 Fersen began to arrange
final details; in May 1791 an offer of colonial concession to
Britain to purchase benevolent neutrality was made, and the
queen wrote to Leopold informing him of the impending flight.
Ill luck and sheer lack of ability ruined a well laid scheme.

Suspicion that the king was planning a flight was growing in
Paris, where the religious conflict had been heightened by the
king's marked preference for non-juring priests. The departure
of the king's aunts in February, outraged at what they regarded
as anticlerical excesses, increased the suspicion, and on 28
February a group of nobles, some armed, invaded the Tuileries
to save the monarchy from a rumoured mob. This *'journée des
poignards'*, was interpreted, incorrectly, as an abortive royalist
coup. When, on 18 April, the king sought to leave Paris to
receive his Easter Communion from a non-juring priest at
Saint-Cloud, the mob turned him back. Now the royal family
was truly the prisoner of Paris. Next day in the Assembly the king
declared he had decided not to go to Saint-Cloud of his own free
will and a circular was sent to European monarchs asserting that
he accepted the Revolution – but from Breteuil they learned
that they should attach no importance to public declarations
and the queen begged Leopold to move 15,000 troops to the
frontier to support Bouillé.

Bouillé concentrated his troops at Montmédy and Fersen, who
had borrowed some £300,000 for the enterprise, completed his
plans. The royal family were to escape to Montmédy, being
joined *en route* by royalist detachments of cavalry posted by
Bouillé. The night of 20 June was eventually chosen for the
flight. Lafayette searched the palace that night on orders from
the mayor, Bailly, but left a door unguarded – the one used by
Fersen on his visits to the queen, and the one through which the
royal family escaped. As the dauphin, dressed as a girl, left the
building, Lafayette rode past, noticing nothing. The extent to
which he was implicated has never been established. But the
family escaped and although recognized at Châlons they were

only stopped at Varennes by the prompt action of a postmaster, Drouet, who closed the bridge against them. Ironically they were within calling distance of a detachment of cavalry – they would have had an escort had they not lost four hours by the way in their heavy *berline* coach, but the troops had retired supposing the king not to be coming that day. A touch of resolution and the king might have been through the barrier and on to Montmédy: there is no doubt what would then have happened. But now it was too late: the monarchy had compromised itself irredeemably.

The flight to Varennes provoked almost a revival of the Great Fear, and a fresh wave of emigration. There was great excitement in Paris but that the monarch was not immediately deposed is a measure of the moderate opinion of the Assembly – perhaps a Leopold would have built up a monarchical party from the moderates. Almost unnoticed in the excitement, the Comte de Provence and his wife escaped that night to Brussels – he was to return with the allied armies in 1814, as Louis XVIII.

There were no telephones or railways, but the National Guard acted so quickly that two officers from Paris reached Varennes less than seven hours after the king. Confirmation of the arrest was not received until the evening of the 23rd. Two days later the fugitives returned, the people showing immense restraint in attempting no violence against them and watching them enter Paris in silence: Marie-Antoinette's hair is said to have turned grey – she was lucky to escape with her life; Favras had died a year before for a far less serious thing.

Despite Robespierre's efforts, the king was not brought to trial – indeed proceedings were opened against those who had 'abducted' him – like Bouillé, who joined the *émigrés* and on 15 July issued a letter warning that he would lead an invasion if the royal family were harmed. Indeed, there was a real danger of foreign intervention for the first time – Leopold issued a circular, urging concerted action, from Padua on 6 July. At home there was revulsion against the monarch and fear of civil war: republicanism now became a force, but its followers were often *sans-culottes* and the Assembly feared a republic would mean

anarchy. They decided to suspend the king until the Constitution
was ready: if he accepted it, he would be restored to full powers.

But the Bourbons learnt nothing from Varennes – the dissim-
ulation continued, and the queen, despite the spies that were
about her, wrote to her brother Leopold on 26 August. 'By
lulling them to sleep . . . we can better outsmart them later'.
She and the *émigrés* can claim some credit for the Declaration of
Pillnitz which the Emperor issued in August, announcing the
possibility of intervention. The plotting continued and led to
war as surely as did the Girondin policies (see page 85). On the
very eve of hostilities (March 1792) she passed French plans of
the campaign to Austria.

She was not the only plotter. There had been Mirabeau; there
was Lafayette; and he was now joined by Barnave. He had been
no friend of the Establishment, but his chivalrous instincts had
been stirred by the queen on the journey back from Varennes.
Fearing a republic would mean anarchy, from July to January
1792 he maintained a secret correspondence with the court
advising the queen to give up her schemes, and the king to accept
the Constitution and work to create a strong executive. The
leading *Feuillants* and Lafayette were privy to this – but the advice was as pointless as Mirabeau's, for the queen continued the
secret diplomacy of the 'Austrian Committee' at the Tuileries.

In 1793, promoting a foreign invasion to defeat the Revolution,
Varennes would have produced full-scale purges: in 1791 it did
much to produce the Massacre of the Champ de Mars. Throughout the spring there was ugly feeling in Paris against the unemployed. An attempt by numerous bodies of wage earners to
enforce a minimum wage and raise wages generally – the biggest
wages movement until 1794 – led the Assembly to adopt the
Loi le Chapelier in June. Varennes turned the discontent into
political channels and the Cordeliers and Jacobin clubs sought
permission to petition in favour of a more republican form of
government. As permission was not granted, Robespierre and the
Jacobins withdrew, but the Cordeliers persisted, and some six
thousand people, many being illiterate, had signed the petition
at a ceremony on the Champ de Mars on 17 July, before Lafayette

and 10,000 National Guardsmen arrived, sent by Bailly. Stones were thrown, the troops fired, and some fifty petitioners were killed. Many arrests were made and the leaders of the Cordeliers Club went into exile for the moment. For the first time the social question had produced an armed political clash within the Third Estate, a clash which was to be repeated with growing intensity in 1848, in 1871 and under the Republics that followed. There was no immediate retaliation, perhaps because the price of bread remained stable and because the mob leaders were driven underground. The Jacobins escaped proscription but remained under a cloud: they split, the *Feuillants*, restricted to active citizens, moderates, supporting the monarchy, left, and for six months the Jacobins were almost in eclipse – perhaps it was Robespierre's vigorous defence of the club that helped it to survive. The massacre destroyed *sans-culotte* confidence in the Constitution and in the Assembly: it destroyed Lafayette's popularity and later when Bailly was executed during the Terror, the *sans-culottes* were to remember their first 'martyrs', and recall that it was he who declared martial law that day and sent the National Guard to shoot on the crowd.

In the next few months Barnave strove hard to stop the Revolution going further towards anarchy, to reconcile the king to the people again before *émigré* activity ruined the chance, and to calm the coalition that was now rising among European powers in hostility to the Revolution. He and the *Feuillants* hoped to revise the Constitution along conservative lines, but the elections for the new Legislative Assembly took place under the existing regulations. Their chief success was a compromise settlement over the *marc d'argent* (see page 65) agreeing to drop this qualification for deputies in return for raising the property qualification for electors – thus reducing the number of active citizens. But it never came into force, for it was overtaken by the Terror which no one could have predicted. Eventually, in September, the king accepted the Constitution and the Constituent Assembly was dissolved – but only Robespierre and Pétion were chaired by the crowds. In the general amnesty the Cordeliers leaders and some royalists were allowed to return.

Elected on a narrow franchise, the new Legislative Assembly
in almost every way lacked the authority of its predecessor.
Although by no means devoid of talent, it was deprived of men
of political experience by the 'self-denying ordinance'. These
men did not stand idly by; they spoke in the Clubs, and soon the
Clubs became almost the rivals of the Assembly. The war question
was debated at length as much in the Jacobins as in the Assembly, and it was the Paris Sections that provided the political
organization to bring down the monarchy. The Constitution
might have survived had the queen and the *émigrés* not intrigued
so much against it, had there been no war, and had Louis's
acceptance of it been sincere. But too many revolutionaries
doubted the king's word and there were many cartoons im-
pugning his good faith. The wonder is that the monarchy survived as much as a year under these conditions. Many deputies,
retiring in September 1791, must have felt the irony of their
position when they recalled the dramatic days of 1789 and
reviewed their efforts to give France stability and constitutional
government. But war was soon to destroy or to imperil much of
their handiwork.

[11] THE COMING OF THE WAR

To understand the origin of the war and the victory of the
Revolution one must look to Europe. Far from precipitating a
war, the Revolution probably prevented another Seven Years'
War from breaking out, for it removed from the scene one of the
principal contestants. When the war did break out, the Revolution discovered a weapon of terrible power – democracy at war
backed by a totalitarian government at home. It was this that
unleashed the full dynamism of the ideas of 1789: they are with
us still.

A century before the Revolution the Turks were besieging
Vienna but, by the end of the eighteenth century, Turkey had

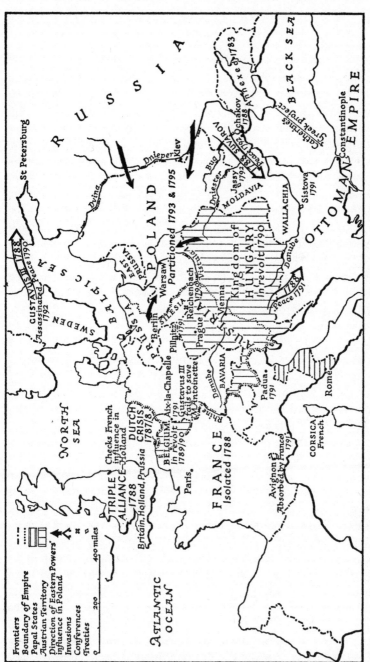

EUROPE ON THE EVE OF THE REVOLUTIONARY WAR   *The Polish imbroglio saves France*

become 'the sick man of Europe' and Catherine the Great's
generals, Potemkin and Suvarov, had been steadily expanding
Russia's southern frontiers at Turkey's expense – the Crimea
was taken in 1783. With the formation of the Austro-Russian
alliance of 1781, Catherine's hope of securing a 'Greek' Empire
centred on Constantinople seemed possible. But other powers
were not prepared to see Russian expansion without securing
'compensation' for themselves. Pitt, desiring to secure British
trade routes across the Levant, and Vergennes, whose influence
with the Porte was considerable, were most likely to oppose the
Russian enterprise. But any hope of joint action was destroyed
by the Dutch crisis and the creation of the Triple Alliance in
1788: lack of money prevented France from making even a show
of force (see page 39) when Prussian troops restored the
Stadtholder. In 1788, Turkey attacked both Austria and Russia
but, after early successes, lost Ochakov to Russia and by the
autumn of 1789 had lost much of the Serbian provinces to
Austria (Belgrade was taken on 6 October, the day Louis XVI
was brought to Paris from Versailles). However, in 1788, taking
advantage of the Turkish War, Gustavus III of Sweden had
invaded Finland and threatened St Petersburg; this war embarrassed Catherine and was not ended until August, 1790. Joseph
II's initial defeats encouraged the Magyar nobles of Hungary and
the Belgians to revolt: the 'Greek Project' was a failure even before the death of Joseph in February 1790.

It was only to be expected that Prussia should seize the chance
to embarrass Austria by encouraging the Belgians in their
revolt and by demanding 'compensation' in Poland for any
Austro-Russian gains in the Balkans. Poland had already
suffered one partition in 1772: she was too well placed and too
weak to avoid being the object of the niceties of eighteenth-
century diplomacy. Prussian troops were massed in Silesia in
August 1789 and it was only the indolence of Frederick William
that prevented the Austrian Empire being struck down on the
death of Joseph II. But the powers withdrew from embarking on
so major a war and met in conference at Reichenbach in July
1790. Leopold was able to settle things in both Hungary and

Belgium. Catherine began to fear that she would be left to fight
Turkey alone and that Leopold would make a separate peace:
she therefore sent a dispatch to Berlin on 26 March 1791 offering
to partition Poland with Prussia and in this way both isolate
Austria and gain Prussian support. Had this been accepted the
whole course of the French Revolution might have been changed
and the world might never have heard of Napoleon. But negotiations for an alliance between Austria and Prussia were already
well advanced and the two monarchs agreed to meet in August
at Pillnitz with the primary intention of sealing their alliance
against Catherine's designs in Poland and the Balkans.

Two things were lacking from this mass of diplomatic movements: France had not entered into the calculations of the
Powers since she was helplessly engaged in internal troubles, and
the Powers had clearly not understood the potential threat that
the Revolution presented to their position. They had been prepared for intervention – just before the Conference of Reichenbach Frederick William had contemplated a joint intervention
with Austria to restore Louis and receive territorial 'compensation'. But Leopold had troubles of his own – he was not blind
to his family and kingly responsibilities but was not prepared to
intervene without very good reason – and the fact that Catherine was urging it was an added reason for caution. However,
early in 1791, inspired by Marie-Antoinette, Gustavus III gave
a lead by establishing himself at Aix-la-Chapelle to aid the French
monarchy – his assassination in March 1792 was a loss to them.
In June Leopold suddenly responded to Prussian suggestions for
intervention: he had received a letter from his sister telling of
the decision to escape to Montmédy. The flight to Varennes
changed the whole course of the Revolution, and ultimately of
European diplomacy. Varennes compelled Europe to look to
France.

That there was no intervention then was due perhaps as much
to the uncertainties of the European situation as to Marie-
Antoinette's concern lest invasion should endanger the royal
family. In July, from Padua, Leopold circularized the Powers on
the possibility of a joint intervention, and made peace with Tur-

key at Sistova in readiness. But the replies were cool and the prudent moderation of the French Assembly together with Catherine's ambitions in the East, led to the Declaration of Pillnitz (27 August 1791) in which Prussia and Austria asserted the principle of intervention provided the Powers agreed to co-operate. As this would never happen, the Declaration was an empty threat: but it did not seem so to the French. When war came in the spring, there was as little cooperation among the Powers as in 1791. Eastern questions were the main things considered at Pillnitz: any war in France was regarded as a secondary matter – perhaps as a source of 'compensation', at the expense of the French monarchy, for Russian gains in the East. There was no lack of a desire to extinguish dangerous revolutionary doctrines; only fear of the consequences of becoming too closely engaged in the West. In January 1792, Leopold suggested he should exchange Belgium for Bavaria; in March, Frederick William informed Catherine of his intention to take 'compensation' in Poland for the expenses of the coming campaign in France. That month Leopold was succeeded by his impetuous son Francis II, anxious to champion the Pope and avenge the insults his aunt had suffered; but, though France declared war in April, Prussia did not mobilize until May. With no common policy or mutual trust, the Powers embarked on a war they supposed would be over in a season: they were no more prudent than the Girondins in their calculations.

The Legislative Assembly which met in October 1791 had a majority of *Feuillants*. Barnave was still their leader, though no longer a deputy, and he hoped to continue the policy of peace and prosperity based on a monarchy loyal to the Constitution. But the queen consistently disregarded his advice, despite the rising tide of anti-Austrian feeling and Lafayette (who had seen Pétion elected mayor of Paris instead of himself) was uneasy about the political situation. Opposing the *Feuillants* were a very small group of extreme Jacobins and a larger group of republicans clustered round Brissot. In the Legislative Assembly called Brissotins, in the succeeding Convention Girondins, because several of them came from the Gironde and Bordeaux, they were

never a party in any definite sense, but a group of politicians
often with financial interests, of the type that became common
in the Third Republic. Their orator was Vergniaud and in Mme
Roland they had a vigorous organizer. Brissot wanted war:
under his skilful direction the group dominated the Assembly and
launched the war.

Conditions at home were difficult that winter. Disturbances
and riots were common – serious food riots over the cost of sugar
occurred in Paris in February. Prices were rising, and the value
of the *assignat* was depreciating seriously – in July 1791 they
were about 85 per cent of their original value, by March 1792
they had fallen to about 59 per cent. This was a reason for war-
mongering, for Belgium would provide an easy victory, since
it was already troubled with revolution, and the *assignat* could
be 'unloaded' on that country, while victory would bring in
bullion and wealth from exploitation.

In certain provinces something like a civil war between the
Revolution and the non-jurors was being waged; and the
Assembly, anxious to restore order, especially as non-jurors
were instructing peasants not to pay taxes, offered a new Oath,
on 27 November 1791, that did not infringe the papal authority,
but did provide severe sanctions against those refusing the oath.
War might deflect attention from such civil strife and induce a
greater unity among Frenchmen.

A fresh wave of emigration occurred in 1791. Artois and Condé
had been organizing counter-revolution since 1789, though few
monarchs took them seriously. By June 1791 Coblenz had
become the *émigrés'* centre, where they lived riotously and
proved an embarrassment. Nearby, at Worms, a more serious
group under Condé trained in preparation for war – they were
some two thousand strong by December 1791. Throughout the
autumn of 1791 the disturbances they promoted were a serious
problem in the south and rumour exaggerated the size of their
army and the gravity of their plots. Their presence was a continual provocation to the Assembly.

On 31 October Provence was ordered to return within three
months or lose his rights to the succession. On 9 November a

decree made traitors of all *émigrés* not returned by 1 January 1792. In fact their most serious disservice to the Revolution was the effect their emigration had on finance, commerce and military discipline. Their secret diplomacy and their loud propaganda both against the Revolution and for foreign intervention, damaged the *Feuillants* and made the continuance of peace unlikely.

Throughout the period of the Legislative Assembly, the king continued the duplicity that he had already demonstrated. Barnave urged him to veto the decrees against the non-jurors and the *émigrés*, in the hope of attracting them back. Louis agreed – it would discredit the Assembly. In November Fersen had drafted appeals to the Powers to intervene. By December rumours of Lafayette's new royalist sympathies and of the activities of the 'Austrian Committee' in the Tuileries, were openly discussed. Despite the spies about her and the security arrangements, the queen was still able to continue her clandestine correspondence. She had an unlooked for ally in Narbonne, the Minister of War, who persuaded the king to support the Order of 14 December 1791 to the Elector of Triers, to disperse the *émigrés* from Coblenz within a month on pain of war. The same day Louis wrote secretly to Breteuil urging that the Emperor should get the Elector to reject so peremptory a demand. But Leopold would not play Louis's game of hurrying France into war in hope of defeat and restoration. The king was encouraging officers to emigrate by obtaining leave and passports for them, and was interrupting the manufacture of munitions. The declaration of war (20 April) was merely the consummation of his policy.

Narbonne rapidly came to the conclusion that morale in the army could best be restored by a limited war on the Rhine, a conclusion that Lafayette supported in hopes of restoring his political position. Narbonne opened negotiations with Prussia and Britain to secure their neutrality – Talleyrand was sent to London and Custine's son was sent secretly to Frederick the Great's veteran general, the Duke of Brunswick, to offer him command of the French forces. Louis secretly disowned, and so ruined, the negotiations – yet Narbonne had hoped to use a

strengthened army to defend the constitutional monarch. Narbonne's policy drove Barnave into retirement; but when in
March Narbonne demanded a purge of the royal household in
favour of the *Feuillants*, Louis amazed everyone by dismissing
him. A Brissotin ministry was forced on the king, for since
January Brissot had been conducting a war of nerves with Austria, demanding she state whether she was friend or foe. Roland
was made Minister of the Interior and Dumouriez, a fierce anti-
Austrian and an old soldier, who, like Narbonne, hoped to strengthen the monarchy, was Minister of Foreign Affairs. Francis II was
now Emperor: war was imminent. Dumouriez made some bold
and imaginative suggestions for an alliance with Britain – surrendering Tobago, helping to liberate the Spanish empire, checking
aggression in Eastern Europe by a Western alliance – proposals
that Talleyrand was to champion at Vienna in 1815 – but Dumouriez's diplomacy was ruined by Breteuil's agents (Goodwin).

Brissot's war propaganda was very popular. He hoped war
would clearly reveal the treason of the crown and that this would
lead to the creation of the republic his supporters so ardently
desired. A short victorious war (he did not contemplate defeat)
would raise French prestige and remove the *émigré* threat by
driving them from the frontiers. The Belgians, he supposed,
would welcome the French as deliverers from Austrian domina-
tion. The war would hold the people together in defence of the
gains of the Revolution and remove attention from bad conditions at home – the Brissotins feared especially demands for
fixed prices and the bogey of the '*loi agraire*', a vague name for
a very real fear that property rights would be overthrown and
land divided out into small lots. Delay would give the Emperor
time to complete his preparations for war so putting France at a
disadvantage. Finally, and perhaps most important of all, his
purpose was the moral, crusading one of national regeneration
and of spreading revolutionary principles, helping others to free
themselves of despotism.

The war question developed into a personal duel between
Brissot and Robespierre speaking in the Jacobin club – it was a
surprisingly courageous stand for Robespierre (or any radical

Jacobin) for war with unpopular Austria was very popular indeed. In January Robespierre warned of the preparations for military dictatorship that Narbonne was making and noted that the court, Lafayette and the *émigrés* all wanted war, 'and is there no connexion between Coblenz and another place not far from where we are?' He urged that France should put her own house in order before launching on a war whose consequences could not be foreseen. The army was not well equipped for war, and this invited defeat – a shrewd forecast that was to be proved only too true. Robespierre was no pacifist, but he wanted security at home and sound planning before embarking on war. The duel aroused deep interest and secured Robespierre's position at the Jacobins, although at the cost of considerable unpopularity for the moment.

There were, then, three groups in France who wanted war – the court, in order to overthrow the Revolution in defeat and be saved from a restoration at the hands of the *émigrés*; Lafayette and the army, who sought employment and political influence; and the Brissotins. Against war were the *Feuillants* and those Jacobins who followed Robespierre. There was scarcely a common thought or motive among them. From January a conflict was imminent, and when Francis succeeded Leopold there was no holding Austria back. On 17 April, three days before France declared war, Thugot told Breteuil that Austria was preparing to march.

In promoting the war no one, the Brissotins least of all, had much thought for the means of war. In France the war quickly concentrated support behind the Revolution, and completed the destruction of the monarchy, and the liberation of the peasant from the last vestiges of feudalism. It developed into the first totalitarian war – ironically in the hands of the very Jacobins who had opposed the war in the beginning. It started as a limited war, but it transcended eighteenth-century limits and became a patriotic war of the people for the people.

Few gained what they hoped from the war – Russia had to share Poland with Prussia and Austria; Prussia gained no Rhenish lands: Austria did not save the monarchy, which perished at

the hands of the people; Marie-Antoinette and the *émigrés* failed
to effect counter-revolution (some *émigrés* trickled back under
Napoleon); the army leaders failed to gain the political influence
they sought and became servants of politicians; and the Girondins found they preferred the monarchy to the republic that
emerged to destroy them.

Further Reading

Some useful ideas can be gained from G. Salvemini, *The French
Revolution 1788 to 1792* (Translated by I. M. Rawson, Cape,
1954). J. Egret, *La pré-révolution française, 1787 to 1788*, (Presses
Universitaire de France, 1962) sums up his work on the period
immediately preceding 1789. For 1789 Georges Lefebvre's *The
Coming of the Revolution* (Translated, R. R. Palmer, Princeton
University Press, 1949) is vital: Frédéric Braesch, *L'année
cruciale, 1789* (Libraire Gallimard, 1950) should also be consulted
– the book was partly inspired by the *dégringolade* of 1940.
Gouverneur Morris, *A Diary of the French Revolution* (ed. B. C.
Davenport, 2 vols, Harrap, 1939) is good reading. O. J. G. Welch
has written a good life of *Mirabeau* (Cape, 1951); other characters
appear in J. M. Thompson's *Leaders of the French Revolution*
(Blackwell, 1929). For diplomatic history, see P. Rain, *La Diplo-
matie Française de Mirabeau à Bonaparte* (Paris, 1947) and A.
Fugier, *La Révolution française et l'Empire napoléonien (Histoire des relations internationales*, tom 4. Paris, 1954). The old
series of the *Cambridge Modern History* contain much useful
material. David Thomson's *Europe Since Napoleon* (Longmans,
1962) should be consulted for the European setting of the Revolution, and Crane Brinton's *A Decade of Revolution, 1789 to 1799*
(Harper, Torchbooks, 1934) is also thought-provoking.

Principal Events 1787 – April 1792

FRANCE

1787–8
Assembly of Notables and
'*révolte nobiliaire*'.

1788

May. Restrictions on the
Parlements

August. Estates General to
be called
27 December. 'Result' of
Council doubles Third
Estate
28 December. Mirabeau's
letter to Montmorin

1789
May. Estates General at
Versailles
4 June. Death of dauphin,
court in mourning at Marly
17 June. 'National Assembly'
claim by Third Estate
20 June. Tennis Court Oath
23 June. Royal Session
26 June. Troop concentration
round Paris begins
27 June. *Réunion des Ordres*
11 July Necker dismissed
12–14 July. Riots in Paris
culminate in the Fall of
the Bastille
July–August. The Great Fear
Many *terriers* burnt

EUROPE

1787–8
Dutch crisis

1788
Turkey at war with Russia
and Austria
June. Sweden at war with
Russia. Triple Alliance of
Britain, Prussia and
Holland
December. Suvarov takes
Ochakov

1789

FRANCE

4 August. 'Abolition' of
  Feudalism
26 August. Declaration of
  Rights of Man and of the
  Citizen
5 October. Women march to
  Versailles
6 October. King returns to
  Paris
2 November. Nationalization
  of Church property
7 November. Decree
  excluding deputies from
  the ministry
November. Louis seeks aid
  against the Revolution
  from Charles IV of Spain
19 December. First issue of
  assignats

1790

4 February. King's speech
  to Assembly
19 February. Favras
  exucuted
11 May. Nootka Sound
  debate
12 July. Civil Constitution
  of the Clergy
14 July. First Feast of
  Federation

September. Suppression of
  Nancy mutiny
October. Fersen begins plans
  for escape of royal family
27 November. Clerical oath
  of loyalty decreed
26 December. King sanctions
  clerical oath

EUROPE

August. Prussian army
  masses in Silesia

6 October. Austria takes
  Belgrade

1789–90

Hungarian nobles in revolt
Belgium in revolt

1790

February. Leopold II
  succeeds Joseph
Spring. Nootka Sound dispute.
  France fails to support
  Spain

July. Convention of
  Reichenbach
August. Russia and Sweden
  make peace

December. Austria regains
  control of Belgium

FRANCE
1791
20 February. Departure of
  king's aunts
28 February. *Journée des
  poignards*
10 March. Pope condemns
  Civil Constitution of
  Clergy

2 April. Death of Mirabeau
18 April. Saint-Cloud affair
16 May. Decree forbidding
  deputies to sit in next
  Assembly
14 June. *Loi le Chapelier*
20 June. Flight to Varennes

17 July. Massacre of Champ
  de Mars

27 August. Declaration of
  Pillnitz
14 September. King accepts
  Constitution
1 October. Legislative
  Assembly
12 November. King vetoes
  decree v. *émigrés*
16 November. Pétion elected
  Mayor in preference to
  Lafayette
19 December. King vetoes
  decree v. clergy

1792

EUROPE
1791

26 March. Russia proposes
  partition of Poland to
  Prussia
Spring. Gustavus III at
  Aix-la-Chapelle

6 July. Leopold circularizes
  the Powers about
  intervention in France
4 August. Treaty of Sistova –
  peace between Austria and
  Turkey
27 August. Declaration of
  Pillnitz

1792
January. Treaty of Jassy –
  peace between Russia and
  Turkey

FRANCE	EUROPE
	7 February. Austro-Prussian alliance
	1 March. Francis II becomes Emperor
	March. Assassination of Gustavus III
	Prussia informs Russia of intention to take
10 March. Brissotin ministry	'compensation' in Poland
	13 April. Austrian troops mobilized in Belgium
20 April. War declared	20 April. War declared
	5 May. Prussia mobilizes
	1793
	Second partition of Poland

PART IV
The Third Phase: 1792–3

[12] THE FALL OF THE THRONE
AND THE FIRST TERROR

A rapid, limited victory would have ensured the position of the
Girondins and ended the Revolution at a point that was quite
favourable to them. An immediate offensive, vigorously pressed
home, would have secured important victories without disturb-
ing too much the delicate balance of European diplomacy –
there were few Austrian troops on the frontiers. But there had
been no real preparation for war. Curiously naive, the Girondins
had expected Austrian and Prussian troops to desert in droves:
when this did not happen, the lack of a war machine was clear
for all to see. The War Office bungled its task and army contractors made fortunes – in many cases fraudulently. Narbonne's
confidence was utterly misplaced, for the army was disrupted by
emigration and its morale was bad. Desertion was common, and
occasionally officers took their men over to the enemy. Discipline
was surprisingly poor – on one occasion it was reported that the
Duc de Biron had to countermand an order for a bayonet charge
because his soldiers voted against it. The generals might be ex-
cused for declining to risk battle with such troops – but they had
schemes of their own.

Dumouriez dreamed of a great sweep across Belgium into
Holland and had disposed three armies in the north and east:
Custine in Alsace, Lafayette at Metz, Rochambeau (who had
commanded the volunteers in America and helped take
Yorktown) at Valenciennes, from which army Biron was to ad-

vance on Brussels. But a 'phoney war' resulted and, when Dillon's troops engaged the Austrians on 29 April, they fled, murdering Dillon on the way. This ended the French offensive, and
the generals met at Valenciennes on 18 May to urge peace talks.
But their concern was political, not military: Lafayette sent an
envoy to the Austrian ambassador indicating he was prepared
to march on Paris and restore the *Feuillants* if Austria would not
invade France.

Perhaps the assassination of Gustavus was the reason why the
allies failed to take advantage of France's defeat. Disunited and
suspicious, their real concern was for Poland: Catherine might
urge them to invade France, but three weeks after Dillon's murder, on the very day the generals met at Valenciennes, 100,000
Russian troops invaded Poland. Perhaps this saved the Revolution: Austria, hoping to exchange the Netherlands for Bavaria,
was in difficulties over assembling her army, fresh from the Turkish war, because of lack of money and opposition in both Belgium
and Hungary. She was not going to launch a great offensive alone
against France. Prussia did not mobilize until May (perhaps this,
too, saved the Revolution). Prussia's army had lost the touch of
Frederick the Great; its artillery was poor, its medical services
non-existent – yet it did not live off the country but carried a
nine-day supply, which meant a camp every nine days and a
cumbersome baggage train resulting in a slow advance at the best
of times. Brunswick, the commander, was a well tried general,
old, but no fool; but he arrived at Coblenz only in July. He knew
how expensive it was to replace a regular army of the Ancien
Régime: one did not take unnecessary risks; furthermore, he
knew that the real purpose of the war was less the defeat of
France – a foregone conclusion – than the acquiring of suitable
territory that would prove useful in subsequent negotiations.
Bouillé had convinced the allies that France was just waiting to
be delivered. Speed, therefore, was not Brunswick's concern –
and the terrain was unsuited to the staging of eighteenth-century
battles. It may have been to forestall any possible ill-effect of his
tardy progress that he issued his famous Manifesto (see page 103).
The diplomats who authorized it seemed to adopt the draft that

Fersen, with the queen's connivance, had made, in a casual moment amidst the splendours of the Imperial Coronation – they little thought they were witnessing the last such scene. Even after the fall of the throne in Paris, Brunswick did not cross the frontier until 19 August.

Reaction in Paris to military collapse was to cry treason, accusing the queen, the 'Austrian Committee' and the generals. As the threat of invasion grew, fear of counter-revolutionary plots, reminiscent of the 'aristocratic plot' of 1789, became widespread, and this was to lead to the great crisis of the summer. But the politicians, though the enemy was knocking at the gates, continued to indulge their personal rivalries – indeed, for the next two years, when the allied threat was turned, it is sometimes difficult to remember, when dealing with Paris, that the city itself was threatened with imminent destruction. Yet the revolutionaries were not alone in this fault – the allied courts were, and remained, similarly disunited; and the Revolution survived to produce the leader who was to humble Europe.

For the immediate future in Paris, the principal rivals were two groups within the Jacobin Club. Robespierre now reaped the reward of his shrewd forecasts during his debate with Brissot about the war, and in the newspaper he edited in May, *Le Défenseur de la Constitution*, he launched an attack on the French generals. Around him grouped the many elements who distrusted *Feuillants* and Girondins alike. As yet this opposition group was not well defined, but in the Convention, elected in September, their unity was cemented and they were called the *Montagnards* because they occupied the high seats in the Assembly. What distinguished them from the Girondins was not social background or ideological disputes, but a greater willingness to accept the reality of a situation and to modify their ideas accordingly. This was particularly true in matters of economic and social policy and, since circumstances led them to an alliance with the *sans-culottes*, they have been called more extreme than the Girondins. But Mathiez may be going too far in representing the struggle between Jacobins and Girondins as at base a great class struggle. Neither Marat, nor Danton of the Cordeliers, was a fol-

lower of Robespierre, but the current of politics drew them together. Lesser figures, however, looked closely to him as leader,
and in the next two years the Robespierrist Jacobins showed the
greatest cohesion of all the revolutionary groups – but they were
not a homogeneous group, especially in the provinces.

The Jacobin campaign to destroy the Girondins has foisted on
History the legend of a Girondin party. Men with similar ideas
do not necessarily make a party; and the Girondins, so far as they
are identifiable, did not act as a group at times of crisis. They
joined Brissot and Roland, in promoting ideological war, and
their great orators, like Isnard, Gensonné and Vergniaud, gave
them great influence in both the Legislative Assembly and the
Convention. From the summer of 1792 they began to neglect
attendance at the Jacobin Club – to their cost – preferring the
Réunion Club, and the *salons* of Mme Roland, Mme Dodun or
Valazé. More deputies among them came from Normandy and
Brittany than from the Gironde. Many were moderately wealthy
lawyers or former civil servants, but they were not all well off,
and before 1792 none of them had any but local influence. But
they tended to lose contact with the poor, and this was to prove
their undoing. Roland's answer to hungry mobs was bayonets.
Their economic ideas were not dissimilar from those of the
Robespierrists, but they pursued a policy of individualism at the
expense of the poor and had a morbid fear of any sort of economic
control by the government. They thought this would lead to the
loi agraire, which they falsely accused the Jacobins of promoting.
Their exclusiveness lost them support (Mathiez accuses them of
forming a 'cave') and Couthon, who joined the *Montagnards* for
just this reason in October 1792, commented: 'The Girondins are
for the republic, because this is the national mandate: but they
are also for aristocracy, because they want to keep their influence,
and to have at their disposal the appointments, the emoluments,
and the financial resources of the republic'.

The Girondins represented the interests of the victors of the
Massacre of the Champ de Mars (see page 77): it was an attitude
that was to play a tragic part in French history by promoting
the far more savage massacres of 1848 and 1871. This distrust of

popular opinion underlined one of their most dangerous traits; many were provincials who dreamed of a Republic in which each Department enjoyed a good deal of self-government. This was not meant to imperil the unity of France, but the Jacobins accused them of it, especially when their appeal to the Provinces to save them from Paris gave rise to the 'federalist revolt' (see page 127). Their fear of Paris centred on their dislike of a dictatorial executive and of the potential power of the *sans-culottes*. Pastor Lasource declared that 'Paris must be confined to her eighty-third share of the total influence, like all the other departments'. These were the '*hommes d'état*', as Marat scornfully called them, who, without preparation, had launched the war to spread the ideals of the Revolution and create the Republic. Yet as conditions worsened, armies retreated and the 'social peril' appeared, they came, by a strange irony, to defend the monarchy they had hoped to destroy – Michelet commented that they were so maladroit that they came to believe themselves royalists.

The 'social peril' that heightened the struggle between Jacobins and Girondins appeared in the towns, especially Paris, and centred on the activities of the *sans-culottes*. Defeated on the Champ de Mars in 1791, they became the essential allies for the Jacobins in the early war years and came near to turning the course of the Revolution when they forced the Jacobins to adopt radical economic measures in September 1793 (see page 134). The sugar riots of February 1792 (see page 83), had given a foretaste of their power, which was well directed through the assemblies of the Sections into which Paris had been divided in 1790 (see page 48).

The literary tradition of the Revolution is sympathetic to the royalists, whose memoirs and letters have sometimes survived. Rarely have letters survived from the *sans-culottes*, who, as the impersonal 'mob', have been the butt of right-wing historians. Recent local studies are now revealing something of the real nature of the urban working population. The *sans-culottes* come somewhere between the bourgeoisie and the true urban proletariat whose struggle for existence left no time for politics. They were not a class but a social group: many earned their living working with their hands, some were master-craftsmen, some small employers, some were quite wealthy. They formed the backbone of the working class movement, acting as a vehicle of propaganda for the illiterate workers under them (reading Marat's and Hébert's newspapers to them), and as the means of organizing sudden concentrations of people whenever necessary. They gained enfranchisement in August 1792, and were keen attenders at their Section Assemblies – in the evenings, for they could not, as a rule, afford to miss a day's work. Sundays were holidays and so were important for political activity and demonstrations.

As they produced neither a Burke nor a Rousseau, it is difficult to determine their ideas with any precision – no one had crystallized a policy for them from the undergrowth of radicalism that inspired them. Certainly, Pétion was quite wrong to speak of them, in April 1793, as 'have-nots as distinct from haves', for they never really challenged private ownership of property – sincerity in the belief in equality was more important to them than income. But their egalitarianism was realistic: equality, if it were to be meaningful, must be fully open to all. In this principle of practical equality (*l'égalité de fait*), which they regarded as complementary to equality of rights, lay the germ of social democracy – and it was this that moderates feared would develop into an attack on property. As early as the summer of 1792, Lange, whom Michelet calls 'with Babeuf, one of the precursors of modern socialism', had written a pamphlet at Lyons advocating national control of foodstuffs and their distribution. In Paris, the abbé Jacques Roux, on 17 May 1792, had demanded the death penalty for speculators and hoarders and urged the control of foodstuffs. Many pamphlets favoured '*le droit à l'existence*' at the expense of property. The Girondins exaggerated this threat of the *loi agraire* – '*Tout homme qui parle de la loi agraire, de partage des terres, est un franc aristocrate* [sic], *un ennemie public, un scélérat à exterminer*'. The threat was no mere phantom.

But their ideas were vague and unformed, in most cases simply a reaction to circumstances. They had done much for the Revolution: they expected some return. Expressed in terms of political theory, this was a demand that society should ensure the happiness of all its members by making all its benefits available to them ('*l'égalité des jouissances*'). This was implicit in Jacques Roux's petition of 23 June 1793: 'Liberty becomes meaningless when the rich exercise the power of life and death over their fellow-creatures'. To men steeped in the writings of the *philosophes* and in the laissez-faire of the *physiocrats*, the idea that governments should actively provide for the livelihood and welfare of citizens was anathema – but the views of Jacques Roux are nearer to those of the mid-twentieth century than are those of his more moderate contemporaries.

Sans-culotte views extended far beyond economic matters. They aspired to a 'puritan' morality which their opponents have entirely concealed. They were austere, homely, family men, who kept their womenfolk close at home. Prostitutes they attacked as parasites, and gamblers as wastrels. Property was no crime among them – if held in moderate amounts – but luxury was bad, for it led to idleness and depravity. They favoured an aggressively simple dress without wig or knee-breeches. Well might Robespierre speak of their simple virtue. They often drank – frequently on empty stomachs – wine stains the minute-books of the Sections more frequently than blood. Obscene literature they tracked down – the vulgarities of Hébert's *Le Père Duchesne* were the common language of artisans. There was idealism amongst them, for they hoped to build a new society of serious, patriotic, virtuous republicans, and they naively called their children after Revolutionary heroes and events.

Many led hard lives and few had developed any economic theory. To end shortages and high prices they naturally advocated the types of control that had been used occasionally on a local basis under the Ancien Régime. To enforce these on a national level was against the views prevailing among the deputies, and might well threaten property. For these, if for no other reasons, no front-rank politician, not even Marat, would lead a crusade on their behalf. When the Jacobins reluctantly accepted many of their ideas, it was because of the conditions of 'siege economy' prevailing in September 1793, and then only as a

temporary measure. But for the vital years at the beginning of
the war, the *sans-culottes* provided the Jacobins with an essential
political weapon; if it proved at times brutal it was scarcely to
be wondered at, for in those unsettled years mass hysteria was
always close to the surface and the fear of an 'aristocratic plot'
was very real. Yet, for the *sans-culottes*, the reality of life was not
the blood of the guillotine, but the queues at the bakers and the
blackmarket.

The military defeats of the summer of 1792 produced a pre-
carious situation: to the cry of treason in high places was added
the fear of counter-revolutionary plots and the need for protection against the 'enemy within'. In May the Legislative Assembly
passed a degree enforcing the registration of aliens and another
against refractory priests – '*les efforts auxquels se livrent constam-
ment les ecclésiastiques non-sermentés pour renverser la Constitution, ne permettent pas de supposer à ces ecclésiastiques la volonté
de s'unir au pacte social*'. Fearing that it might be used against the
Assembly, a decree was also passed disbanding the king's personal bodyguard. Then the Girondins demanded a decree establishing a camp at Paris for 20,000 National Guardsmen from the
Provinces (*fédérés*). This would release the troops in Paris for
the front and would bring a reliable force through which the
Girondins could control on the one hand the Paris National
Guard, already showing signs of royalism, and on the other the
Sections, whose influence they had reason to fear because of the
bad economic conditions.

The king, confident of the early arrival of the Prussians,
sanctioned the disbandment of his bodyguard, but, not surprisingly, the Paris National Guard petitioned against the proposed
camp in what is called the 'petition of 8,000'. The camp was
vetoed – for it would have made Louis the prisoner of the
Girondins. The day of the petition, Roland, as Minister of the
Interior, published an insolent letter urging the king to withhold
his veto. '*Je sais que le language austère de la vérité est rarement
accueilli près du trone*'. Louis's prompt reply was to dismiss the
Girondin ministry and veto both the decree against the priests
and that calling the *fédérés* to Paris. A *Feuillant* ministry was

31364

appointed: had it pursued vigorous action, the throne would have been saved. Instead, the Girondins were allowed to profit by a demonstration that damaged the political position of the monarch.

20 June was the anniversary both of the Tennis Court Oath and of the Flight to Varennes. Some form of demonstration was to be expected, but it is still not clear to what extent the Girondins actively organized it. Certainly Pétion, the Girondin Mayor of Paris, permitted the demonstration to take place; but there was much ill-feeling among the *sans-culottes* at the rising cost of living and it is scarcely surprising that a move to present a petition should begin in the two most politically active faubourgs, the Saint-Marcel, under Alexandre of the Gobelins Section, and the Sainte-Antoine, under Santerre. The citizens paraded under arms and in the evening gained access into the Tuileries although the king, expecting an attack, had doubled the guard. For two hours a constant stream of citizens trooped passed the king chanting slogans – '*A bas le véto!*' and '*Rappel des ministres patriotes*'. Eventually Pétion arrived and after speeches the crowd withdrew. The king behaved with exemplary courage, for which he has been given too little credit. He donned a cap of liberty and drank the health of the nation, but made no concessions. Bonaparte, aged 22, witnessed the scene; 'What a – – –', he is reported as saying, 'How could he have permitted this rabble to enter! If he'd only have turned the cannon on them and shot down five or six hundred, the rest would have run!'

But the Girondins, whether or not they planned it all, failed to take advantage of the demonstration. Instead, it may have worked against them, for there was considerable disgust at the treatment of the king and some minor insurrections – in Brittany the Marquis de la Rouerie planned a rising to coincide with the Prussian invasion. In the south an incipient civil war had been brewing all the spring – the Jacobins of Marseilles had put down counter-revolution at Arles. Rumours of royalist risings merely gave apparent substance to the rumours of a widespread royalist plot. The fear of this plot, the bad conditions and the military defeats all help to explain the hysteria in Paris that summer: 10 August and the September Massacres were no isolated

events, for their roots go deep into the 'revolutionary mentality'.

Hoping to profit by the royalist feeling in the country, Lafayette, without permission, returned to Paris on 28 June intending to rouse the capital to defend the king, destroy the democracy
of the Sections and dissolve the Jacobin Club. It was the queen
who made the king reject his help, for she neither trusted nor
liked him. But his action had reinforced Robespierre's talk of
disloyal generals and it had shown that the Paris National
Guard was not without royalist sympathies. Despite their fear
of a Cromwell, the Girondins refused to proceed against Lafayette – indeed, like revolutionaries before them, they were drift-
ing towards the monarchy, for it gave them security against the
'democracy of the Sections' that might overwhelm them with
the *loi agraire*. A month later, Brissot actually went as far as to
denounce republicanism.

The *Feuillants* ministry, under heavy pressure, resigned on
10 July and Louis was compelled to accept the Girondins back
again. Next day a state of emergency was proclaimed – *'la
patrie est en danger'*. Carnot, the future 'organizer of victories'
might say, 'From the moment when danger exists, everyone is
a soldier', but the declaration of emergency was a mild affair
when the dangers facing the country are considered. It took the
Jacobins to organize national resistance. The Girondins entered
into secret correspondence with the king – yet at the celebrations
of 14 July there were no cries of *'vive le roi'* (he wore a breast-
plate), but of *'vive Pétion'* and *'Pendez Lafayette'*. The king's
advisors were well aware of approaching crisis, but Louis refused
to flee to Lafayette at Compiègne (he had no wish to become a
hostage); he banked on the arrival of the Prussians, and the
queen urged the publication of the Brunswick Manifesto. He also
banked on bribery and the vacillation of the Girondins, as well
as on armed support in Paris.

On 11 July all citizens possessing pikes were drafted into the
National Guard – thus the Assembly transformed the Paris
force into a truly citizens' Guard. This helped the Jacobins.
They were acutely conscious that the Girondins were planning

to crush them. For this reason they determined to save themselves, and the Revolution, by an alliance with the *sans-culottes*.
Two factors turned the tide in their favour. The first was the
arrival of the *fédérés*, for a camp had been allowed at Soissons.
They had to pass through Paris – many without shoes or stock-
ings, some without even a shirt – and they stayed, billeted on
citizens, for the celebration of 14 July. As early as 11 July
Robespeirre had published an address to the *fédérés* – if the
Girondins hoped they would help them against their rivals, it was
the Jacobins who organized the *fédérés* into a valuable force for
overthrowing the monarchy. On 25 July, the Brest *Fédérés*
arrived and on the 30th, fresh from their victory at Arles, came
the Marseillais, singing the song that Rouget de Lisle had composed, which was to become the National Anthem. They were
quartered on the faubourg Sainte-Antoine and prompt Jacobin
efforts stopped royalist efforts to bribe them. They presented
petitions demanding the king's deposition and the *sans-culottes*
fraternized with them. But on 27 July only fourteen of the forty-
eight Sections could be trusted to back an insurrection. An organizing committee of the Sections was set up that day and it maintained close contact with a secret directory formed among the
fédérés – Santerre, Alexander and the abbé Roux, as well as
Robespierre and Marat, were prominent in planning the coup
that was in preparation.

The second factor which made their task easier was the publication of the Brunswick Manifesto, whose terms were known in
Paris on 28 July – if the Tuileries were again invaded or royal
persons insulted, it declared, the allies would take '*une vengeance
exemplaire et à jamais memorable, en livrant la ville de Paris à une
execution militaire et à une subversion totale*', furthermore should
the royal family be taken from Paris, the places on their route
would be similarly treated if they did not stop the king's captors.
It was confidently issued, but it did not strike that terror that
was intended; instead it welded the Sections together, for it
seemed to confirm the royalist plot they feared. By 3 August,
forty-seven out of forty-eight Sections had petitioned for deposition. When the Assembly threw out a motion of censure on

Lafayette for his previous conduct, the Sections had their sign to act lest the royalists carry out a coup to forestall them – besides an attempt had been made on Robespierre's life on 8 August. On the 9th a Revolutionary Commune superseded the official Commune and gained control of the capital. It was at this point that Danton returned after some days at Arcis-sur-Aube. Subsequently, he boasted of having instigated the rising of 10 August, but the evidence for it is sparse – Robespierre had been more concerned with the organizing committee of the Sections (though his influence may have been less than Mathiez suggests). But Danton's influence as a politician was never in doubt and he may have played an important part in gaining the cooperation of the Marseillais - yet his absence is odd, and Lafayette asserted that among the massive bribes of the Court, 50,000 écrus went to Danton. On the night of the insurrection he was certainly active – not so his friend Camille Desmoulins, for as Mathiez puts it, '*Si Camille Desmoulins était sorti avec un fusil, ce n'était pas pour s'en servir*'.

A show of the courage of 20 June might have saved the king, for he had done more than bribe and wait for the Prussians. The Tuileries was well guarded and secret passages had been dug to allow in more troops unobserved. Against an undisciplined mob, they were confident; indeed, they expected to greet the Prussians as masters of Paris, not prisoners of the Assembly or the Sections. But Mandat de Grancey, the royalist commander of the National Guard at the Tuileries was murdered and replaced by Santerre. This paralysed the defence. Furthermore, the king and his family were persuaded to go to the Assembly when the crowds converged on the palace. Many of the National Guard went over to the revolutionaries, who, led by the Marseillais, penetrated the courtyard and advanced to fraternize with the Swiss Guards, As they did so, they were raked by the guns of the Swiss. Cries of treachery, as at the Bastille, were raised and the attack began without quarter. The Swiss and remaining royal troops put up a spirited defence until the king sent word to cease fire. But the crowd continued the fight for some time and six hundred of the Swiss were killed. They were the king's most

loyal troops: they had been shamefully treated. The lion raised to
their memory on the shores of lake Lucerne is small recompense:
in contrast, the three hundred Parisian *sans-culottes* wounded and
the families of those killed received pensions.

Organized by the Jacobins, the Sections had overthrown the
monarchy and passed sentence on the Assembly. The presence of
the *fédérés* gave them in some measure the right to speak for
France. Mirabeau might write complex and fruitless Notes to the
Court: it was the Jacobins who acted. Yet the Girondins, who
had hindered rather than helped the insurrection which had
produced the republic that they had once advocated, remained
in power for the next ten months. The Revolutionary Commune,
unknown men, perhaps overawed by the oratory in the Assembly,
was inhibited from pressing its advantage, despite Robespierre's
urgings: it was content to see a Girondin ministry firmly established with an Executive Council to ensure effective government.
Danton was accepted as the leading minister of this Council. He
was made Minister of Justice – perhaps as Condorcet said, to
protect the Girondins from popular distrust; perhaps because of
his importance for 10 August; certainly because of his influence
with the Sections. The Jacobins were not yet in power – perhaps
they feared the consequences of too close an alliance with the
sans-culottes, and they knew that in the provinces the Girondins
were popular; perhaps, also, they had no wish to risk a breakdown of government by further action, for Brunswick was on the
frontier.

The Assembly only suspended the king, leaving the decision
as to his fate to a new Convention to be elected on universal
male suffrage (thus ending the distinction between 'active' and
'passive' citizens, drawn by the 1791 Constitution). This satisfied
the majority of Frenchmen. But in view of the perilous situation
vigorous action was needed. Municipalities were given the right to
arrest suspects and a decree banished non-juring priests (though
this was without effect in some provinces). Feudal land dues (*droit
réel*) for which no title deed existed were abolished without compensation (see page 57), though this was perhaps intended more to
strike at nobles than help the peasant. But by a decree of 2 Septem-

ber, to 'bind the country people to the Revolution', sequestrated
émigré land was to be sold in small lots to help more peasants
purchase land. Unemployment and food shortages were serious
problems in the towns. The Commune put the Paris unemployed
to work on fortifications. In Lyons, with 30,000 silk workers unemployed, and at Tours, price fixing was adopted. Already the
outlines of the Terror of 1793 were being sketched. On 20 August,
the Jacobin Lindet wrote to his brother, '*La Révolution nous
mène loin. Garde la loi agraire*'.

To the problems of food supply and bad conditions were added
military dangers and uncertainties on the home front. On the
very day Brunswick crossed the frontier, 19 August, Lafayette,
having failed to get his army to return to Paris to overthrow the
Jacobins, deserted to the Austrians. They imprisoned him at
Olmütz – a romantic figure whose firm republican views were
seriously embarrassed by his fruitless efforts to save the monarchy.
He was to gain another place in Revolutionary history, when in
1830, as the patron of the Republic he was now betraying, he
placed France into the hands of another King of the French.

Brunswick's advance was not accelerated by the fall of the
throne. Heavy rain and dysentery were additional causes of delay.
On 23 August Longwy fell and on 2 September Verdun was
delivered up to the invaders by the royalists. There was no
major fortress left now between Brunswick and Paris. On 8
September he entered the Argonne Forest. Vigorous measures of
national defence were adopted; horses, arms, church bells and
plate were requisitioned and, despite its implications, on 4
September the requisitioning of price-controlled grain and fodder
for the army was ordered. Danton put himself at the head of the
call to patriotism and at this time well deserved Michelet's title
of the 'voice of the Revolution and of France'. On the morning
that the news of the siege of Verdun was received, he declared in
a great speech to the Asssembly: 'The tocsin which is about to be
rung is no alarm-signal; it sounds the charge against the enemies
of the country . . . *il faut de l'audace, encore de l'audace, toujours
de l'audace, et la France est sauvée*'. It was such leadership that
saved France.

But there was no abatement of counter-revolutionary activity, and much resistance to requisitioning. In La Vendée, an insurrection gave a foretaste of the serious rising of the following March. Rumours of royalist plots were legion. 10 August had relieved the political crisis a little, but it had not brought security. Violent riots were a feature of that disrupted summer – the fall of Longwy provoked a massacre of imprisoned priests at Cambrai. At Paris, Santerre, newly commanding the now 'democratic' National Guard, was warned on 11 August, *'que l'on forme le projet de se transporter dans toutes les prisons de Paris pour y enlever tous les prisoniers, et en faire une prompte justice'*. Similar reports were made later in the month. On 17 August, to avoid any such action, the Assembly appointed a popular tribunal, elected by the Sections, to try 'suspects' and those responsible for the 'ambush' of patriots at the Tuileries on 10 August. But its deliberations were slow – a speedier instrument of public safety was needed to satisfy popular sentiment. The prisons were overcrowded and ill-guarded: a mass escape was feared at the very time that volunteers were leaving the capital in great numbers for the front. The prisons were also the source of many counterfeit *assignats*, whose production added to economic troubles. A house-to-house search for arms, which Danton had ordered for the end of August in the hope of getting guns, and perhaps removing them from 'suspects', added to the general excitement. Fear of the aristocratic plot, always near the surface in the early years of the Revolution, welled up to present an image of the prisons full of storm troopers waiting for the moment of a royalist coup. There was no need for popular feeling to be directed towards the prisons. Marat's style as a journalist was extravagant, and he had frequently urged a slaughter of aristocrats in order to save the Revolution. But there is no need to look to him, or to any single man, as the evil genius of the September Massacres: what Lefebvre has called the revolutionary 'collective mentality' was already there.

But there may have been some particular political motivation. The Revolutionary Commune, through the reorganized National Guard, controlled Paris, but as the Girondins gained confidence, its very future was in jeopardy. The Jacobins could not afford to permit this, which may explain why Robespierre demanded the arrest of those Girondins responsible for a 'conspiracy in favour of Brunswick' – Carra had even thought to put either Brunswick or the Duke of York on the throne. Danton prevented any proscription, but angry rumours circulated that the Girondins sought to escape the predominance of Paris, the Commune, Sections and Prussians by removing the Assembly to a provincial city. 'Beware, Roland, of taking flight', said Danton, who would have been powerless away from Paris, 'Be careful lest the people hear you'. Jealous of Danton and of the Commune, Roland sought to destroy the latter by requiring new elections to it. His motion was rescinded on 2 September, when the Commune's *comité de surveillance* was reconstituted, and Marat became a member. Roland's move had failed, but it added to the tension at a crucial time. 'Everything we have done has been sanctioned by the people', cried Tallien in the Assembly, 'if you strike at us, strike also at the people who made the Revolution on 14 July, consolidated it on 10 August and will uphold it'.

The massacres began on 2 September, when a group of refractory priests were murdered at the Abbaye prison, and spread rapidly, continuing spasmodically until 6 or 7 September. Tribunals were formed which condemned prisoners to summary execution or released them. (Maillard, hero of the Bastille and the October Days, was important at the Abbaye tribunal.) Little seems to have been done to check the killings; Danton let things ride – perhaps the Assembly half believed in the prison plot. Later, Roland commented: 'I know that the people, terrible though its vengeance may be, yet displays in it a sort of justice'. There were some 2,800 prisoners in the nine prisons affected and of these between 1,100 and 1,400 were killed in the five days and perhaps 1,500 spared by the tribunals. Only 37 were women. The killings were mostly speedy – though special mutilations were reserved for the body of the queen's friend the Princesse de Lamballe. In the circumstances, it is surprising there were not more obscenities committed. Of the victims only about a quarter were priests and political prisoners: the rest were common criminals (feared as the 'brigands' who would have massacred Parisians had the 'plot' been allowed to break).

The men who carried out the massacres, the *Septembriseurs*, were few in number; there were some *fédérés* among them, but most were *sans-culottes*. They were ordinary men reacting to a common danger in an atmosphere of hysteria; they were not *'buveurs de sang'*. Fabre d'Eglantine in November identified them as *'les hommes du 10 Aout'*.

The wife of Julien de Drôme was jubilant that the people were 'avenging the crimes of three years of the basest treachery', and in the fever of patriotism of the moment, France did not repudiate the massacres. Later, the Girondins made great play over the circular, signed by Marat and others, issued by the *comité de surveillance*, on 3 September, urging the provinces to come to the aid of Paris, eliminating counter-revolution on the way: but it had a small circulation, and murders in the provinces continued as they had been doing in the previous month. Europe reacted violently: August and September changed many supporters of the Revolution into opponents, and the counter-revolutionary propaganda, representing the Jacobins as bloodthirsty, destructive hooligans, was launched. History has never forgiven the September massacres – perhaps because they happened in France; other massacres are forgotten. However, the 'enemy within' was defeated, and there was no chance now of a restored monarchy. In a sense, the *Septembriseurs* had saved the Revolution for History.

[13] THE JACOBIN COUP D'ÉTAT

While blood was being spilt in Paris, Brunswick was conducting complex manoeuvres in the Argonne Forest. Eventually on 19 September he lay behind Kellermann and Dumouriez, cutting off their retreat. On 20 September, ignoring best military advice, Frederick William ordered Brunswick to march upon the French.

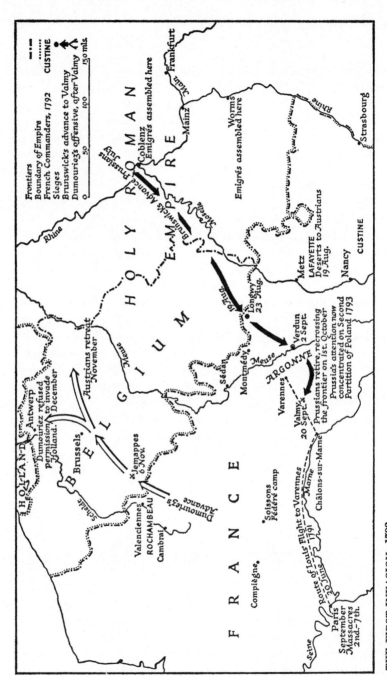

THE FIRST INVASION, 1792

The result was the famous cannonade at Valmy. Today, historians allow it little place, but in 1792, exaggerated into a great
victory, it generated a flood of enthusiasm that saved the Republic. Goethe, who witnessed the firing, noted that a new era had
dawned. The French cannon checked Brunswick's advance and
he retired, in good order. Dumouriez hesitated and sent messages
to the Prussians, hoping for an alliance against Austria. But the
news of the declaration of the Republic ended all chance of negotiations and a much chastened Frederick William, with Brunswick
and 17,000 men, retreated on 1 October. They were concerned
for their Polish interests. The retreat was no defeat, but it saved
the Republic and changed the apparent course of history.

Advances took place on all fronts – Custine took Mainz and
pushed on to Frankfurt; Anselme took Nice, and Montesquiou
was hailed as the deliverer of Savoy. In Belgium the Austrians
withdrew, and on 6 November, pursuing his aim of invading
Holland, Dumouriez won the first great victory of the war at
Jemappes. It was a bloody battle won by mass attacks of the
sans-culottes volunteers: more than Valmy it showed the power
of the Revolution. It seemed the first fruits of Girondin ideological warfare, and on 16 November the Convention flouted international law by declaring the Scheldt free to navigation. On the
19th came the famous 'Fraternity and Assistance' decree:
*'fraternité et secours à tous les peuples qui voudront recouvrer leur
liberté'*. It was now France against the world. Soon Savoy, Nice
and the Rhineland were demanding union with France: apparently the Girondin ideal of achieving 'natural frontiers' was to be
realized. No wonder the Girondins remained in power. But the
expense of 'liberation' was great and led them to the famous
'Guerre aux châteaux, paix aux chaumières' decree of 15 December,
which instituted revolutionary councils in occupied areas to
impose revolutionary measures, like abolishing feudalism and
securing of nobles' lands. The decree brought in much needed
money and allowed devalued *assignats* to be unloaded on the
'liberated'; it also brought great ill-feeling, especially when anticlerical measures were adopted in Belgium. Robespierre predicted
that it would cause so much disaffection against the French that

annexation would be the only answer. By March 1793 Savoy, Nice, Belgium and the Rhineland had been annexed: the Revolution had become an aggressive force. Yet at the same time Dumouriez failed to persuade the Convention to agree to an invasion of Holland in December 1792; and the volunteers, having saved the Republic, began to return home, supposing the campaign to be over.

Meanwhile, the allies were even less united after Jamappes. Conscious of Russia's strength in Poland, Prussia considered withdrawing from her alliance. To keep Prussia in the French war, Catherine hastened the Second Partition of Poland, signing a formal treaty with Prussia on 23 January 1793 – but she kept the main part of her army in Poland, and Austria was left to bear the brunt of war in the west with as yet no 'compensation' in Poland. Once again the allies' failure to cooperate ensured the future of the Republic. And the amazing change in the military position permitted the politicians to relax the emergency measures of the summer.

The elections for the Convention had been held in the crisis of the September Massacres. Universal suffrage had not been a success: there were many abstentions, others were refused the franchise, and the method of indirect voting gave a considerable weight to the wealthy. In Paris, where voting was held publicly in the Jacobin Club, all but one of the twenty-four deputies returned were Jacobins – Robespierre, Danton, Camille Desmoulins, Marat, even the Duc d'Orléans, now Philippe Égalité. In the provinces, the Girondins, as the men associated with national defence, had a big following and many delegates were returned. These formed the new ministry. Between the two rival groups was a third known as the 'Plain', whose support was necessary for a majority and who would support the 'national cause'. In social composition, the Convention was broadly similar to the Assembly it replaced (190 were members of both); there were several former aristocrats, 48 clergy and 2 working men, but the majority were urban bourgeoisie, many being lawyers.

It met on the day of Valmy and on 21 September declared a Republic *une et indivisible*. Next day it proclaimed 1792 as

Republican Year One. Everywhere symbols of the monarchy disappeared, '*citoyen*' replaced '*Monsieur*' as the normal mode of address, and a simple style of dress was fashionable. As the military situation eased, the emergency controls and regulations were withdrawn and in November the sale of *émigré* land was suspended. On 8 December, unlimited freedom of commerce was decreed. The Jacobins did not protest against this rejection of *sans-culottes* ideas, for they were no more in favour of them than their rivals. In November, amid the general approbation of the Convention, the young Saint-Just declared '*Je n'aime point les lois violentes sur le commerce. On demande une loi sur les subsistences! Une loi positive là-dessus ne sera jamais sage*'. Any hopes of a general price control were belied: it needed a still greater crisis than that of the summer for the *sans-culottes* to achieve this aim.

But the leading figures of the Convention were not united in the face of the difficulties that confronted the new Republic. The Girondins far from promoting the 'unity of the Republic', conducted a virulent campaign against the Jacobins who had combined with the *sans-culottes* to bring down the throne in a crisis that had threatened their own position. Personal enmity is the most likely explanation of their conduct – best seen in the Rolands, who could not forgive Danton for stealing their thunder in August. But, though so much of the Convention's time was consumed by the rivalry of Girondins and Jacobins, one must remember the sound work done for education policy and legal reforms that laid a foundation for Napoleon's Codes.

Within days of its opening, the Convention witnessed a full-scale attack on Robespierre and Marat as budding dictators. Tallien's appeal to 'concern ourselves with the safety of the state and leave individuals alone', was ignored. The Girondins' lack of restraint in their personal attacks eventually lost them the support of the Plain, whilst Robespierre grew in stature as he deflected the continued attacks made against him. Their greatest miscalculation was to antagonize Danton, who might well have promoted that unity that the Convention lacked, and who did not share Robespierre's hatred of his rivals. Apart from personal

attacks they allowed their distrust of Paris to supply ammunition to their opponents, as when they tried, unsuccessfully, to
have a departmental guard provided to protect the Convention,
apparently from the Parisians. By the end of September the
Jacobins were accusing them of 'federalism' which would undermine the unity of the Republic. By the end of November, their
power was waning and a moderate Girondin Mayor of Paris was
flanked by Chaumette and Hébert, two extreme Jacobins, as
procureur and assistant *procureur*. The Jacobins controlled Paris:
it was the situation of the summer. To strengthen their positions
Girondins sought allies among the royalists, Jacobins among the
sans-culottes. Then the Jacobins accused their rivals of deliberately postponing the trial of the king. A British observer commented:
'Roland and Brissot's party are certainly struggling to save the
king in order to humble Robespierre'.

The debate on the king's trial began in November. An amazing
discovery precipitated the matter – an iron chest was found at
the Tuileries and inside was a mass of incriminating documents
revealing Louis's double-dealing, royal contact with France's
enemies and attempts at bribery, together with Mirabeau's
royalist schemes. Immediately, Mirabeau ceased to be a hero;
his bust was draped and his body was later to be dragged from
the Panthéon to make room for Marat's. The king's guilt was
obvious; the only problem was the sentence. Yet the Girondins
still sought to avoid a trial – perhaps they feared a royalist
rising, or a really vigorous attack by the allies. But, as Robespierre demonstrated in two great speeches in December, their
position was untenable. It was they who claimed the credit for
10 August; they who regained power because of it – and the Convention existed because the throne and the Constitution of 1791
had been overthrown. 'If the king is not guilty, then those who
dethroned him are', Robespierre declared. A trial, indeed, was
unnecessary and would serve as an opportunity for royalist
propaganda – the king had declared war on the Revolution and
been defeated by it: '*il faut le condamner sur-le-champ à mort, en
vertu d'une insurrection*'. After two months' debate the Girondins
were forced to place the king on trial before the eyes of the world.

But in France, for all the counter-revolutionary activity of the royalists, no serious attempt was made to save the king. And Europe, soon to demand the death of the regicides, let events take their course.

In his defence, Louis denied treason (which was untrue) and challenged the Convention's right to try him – but the Convention was elected to produce a new constitution to replace the one he had betrayed and was vested with full powers. His final plea of royal inviolability was scarcely reasonable. Any trial of a king is illegal to a monarchist: but France was no longer a monarchy and the king had become a private citizen. Few questioned that the king was guilty; the surprising thing is that the deputies were anxious to save his life. The Girondins resorted to obstruction and called for an appeal to France on the question of the king's punishment. On 14 January 1793 the Convention by a practically unanimous verdict, voted that the king was guilty. A heavy majority rejected the proposal of those wishing to refer the problem of the king's fate to the people (the *appelants*), and the Girondins, fearing political defeat, pressed the case for a reprieve. This was rejected by a majority of sixty: the Girondins had not voted as a party; the leaders voted for death, their followers were in the minority. Roland had feared another massacre, for there was considerable agitation in the Sections, but the only victim was Le Pelletier, assassinated on 20 January by a royalist who mistook him for Philippe Égalité, the king's cousin who had voted for the king's death. To the last, the royalists had hoped for a reprieve and had spent vast sums in bribes – Ocariz, the Spanish chargé d'affaires, spent 2 million livres. The final vote seems to have taken them by surprise.

The execution took place on 21 January. The $2\frac{1}{2}$-mile route from the Temple prison to the Place de la Révolution, was lined by National Guardsmen; the crowds were surprisingly calm. Louis's death did much to redeem his earlier errors – it aroused pity and gave the royalists a martyr: yet most of France received the news in silence. For the Jacobins, it was a triumph both against their rivals and against counter-revolution. There was now no chance of compromise, and Europe could avenge Louis's death only by crushing the Revolution: the Jacobins had forced upon France a choice the significance of which leading politicians well understood – Louis had died so that the Revolution should go forward beyond the point at which the Girondins had hoped to stop it.

Neither Austria nor Prussia, it seems, correctly estimated the real threat to the king's life, and both feared disorders at home should they embark on the strain of determined war to crush France. In any case, the Polish imbroglio inhibited them – the Second Partition was not completed until September 1793, and the following year a revolt in Cracow once more withdrew forces from the west. It was no wonder that the Third Partition followed in 1795.

But by the spring a formidable coalition faced France. War was declared on Holland, England and Spain – 'If we had hesitated, the Jacobins would have seized power', Brissot admitted to David Williams, an Englishman in Paris. In midsummer there were 100,000 allied troops in the north-east, almost as many on the Rhine and a sizeable force of Sardinians and Spaniards in the south. The last act of the Girondin tragedy was to be set against the background of foreign invasion and internal revolt. Once more the Republic was saved by the stupidity of its enemies abroad: sure of victory, they failed to unite or to push home their advantage. The death of the king had not altered their tactics or policies.

The Jacobins were convinced that their rivals could not save the country from the new peril and, as much to save themselves as France, they turned once more to the *sans-culottes*. In the Sections, with continuing fears of an aristocratic plot, there was considerable activity and many demanded the expulsion from the Convention of the *appelants*. Also the social question was forcing itself upon politicians, indeed, the cost of living was to play a big part in the overthrow of the Girondins. The *assignats* had declined to 50 per cent of their original value by February 1793; they were to decline further both because of the action of Pitt and international bankers in the exchanges and because of over-issue in France – indeed, the printers struck against the excessive overtime needed to print the new issues. Food was scarce. A British fleet in the Straits of Dover interrupted grain supplies from the Baltic and it was not easy to get local areas to release their grain to the towns. The Lyons workers demanded price control, and the Paris Commune did regulate the price of bread. In three years retail prices of some foodstuffs, especially sugar had risen by as much as 100 per cent. Naturally, the poor wanted 'something done', for it was they who formed the levies for the front. In February, after a levy of 300,000 men had been ordered, there was a wholesale invasion of grocers' and chandlers' shops where the crowd forced the sale of goods at a low price. This *taxation populaire*, as it was called, was not exactly shop-lifting, and does not appear to have been organized, although the prices charged were remarkably similar in different parts of Paris. But it savoured too much of the *loi agraire*, and Santerre quickly restored order. It was clear that the new constitutional proposals that Condorcet had just laid before the Convention had failed to satisfy the *sans-culottes*: they wanted food.

Prices continued to rise and police reports continued to indicate that the *sans-culottes* believed a purge of the Convention would lead to more effective food supplies, energetic measures against hoarders and profiteering army contractors, and price regulation. Jean Varlet, and the abbé Jacques Roux, whose followers were called the *enragés*, played a great part in forming opinion among the Sections. They wanted general price control throughout France and the use of the *assignats* as the sole legal tender. Their petitions were so violent that even Marat declared them subversive. The Jacobins would not yet accept their economic programme, but they could not afford to allow the *enragés* to seize control of the Sections.

Things almost came to a head in the March Days, following news of reverses in Belgium. Feeling in Paris was reminiscent of the previous September; Danton called for volunteers and vigorous measures – 'We are here to act, not to trade in tittle-tattle'. On 10 March a *Tribunal Révolutionnaire* was appointed to forestall massacres and to deal with all counter-revolutionary activity '*contre la liberté, l'égalité, l'unité et l'indivisibilité de la*

République'. The previous day the offices of several Girondin newspapers had been attacked and an insurrectionary committee threatened to march on the Convention to expel the *appelants*. They were prevented by Santerre's National Guard and the Brest *Fédérés*. On 18 March death was decreed for anyone advocating the *loi agraire*, but next day death was also decreed against all rebels in arms and on the 28th the draconian laws against *émigrés* were codified – captured *émigrés* were to be executed and their lands sequestrated. On 6 April the first *Comité de Salut Public*, dominated by Danton, was created to supervise and invigorate the executive: '*Ce comité délibérera en secret; il sera chargé de surveiller et d'accélérer l'action de l'administration confiée au conseil exécutif provisiore.*'

Danton's demand for further levies in March led to serious trouble in many areas: it precipitated the rising in La Vendée. These peasants were neither royalists nor supporters of the Ancien Régime – but they were angry at the severity of the local Jacobin administration and were incensed at the treatment of refractory clergy. It proved the most serious rising of all, for it was well directed, first by the commoners, like Cathelineau, son of a mason and Jean Cottereau, the former smuggler and leader of the *Chouans*, and later by royalist nobles. As it was on the coast, there was always a fear that the British navy would supply help and land an *émigré* army; the revolt developed into a bitter civil war, typified by the greatest cruelties on either side, that lasted for as much as seven years. Soon the rebels were able to muster armies of 30–40,000 men: against them the government could put only untried levies that did not know the countryside. Had the rebels advanced, they might have threatened Paris; but they refused to become a regular army and returned home after each alert. It was this that saved Paris from them.

While La Vendée broke out into rebellion, the news from the front became disastrous. Dumouriez, who blamed the mismanagement of the Convention for the failure of his offensive in Holland, was beaten by the Austrians at Neerwinden on 18 March. He concluded an armistice with them, with the idea of marching on Paris to restore 'Louis XVII' and the Constitution of 1791.

Danton himself failed to secure the general's continued allegiance and Dumouriez handed over the commissioners sent to arrest him to the Austrians. But his army refused to support him, so, like Lafayette before him, he deserted to the Austrians, taking with him the Duc de Chartres, who was to become the King of the French into whose hands Lafayette delivered the still-born republic of 1830. For some days no one was sure of the loyalty of the army. A second invasion was imminent, and the 'noble Duke of York' with his 10,000 men newly arrived in the Netherlands advanced to lay siege to Valenciennes. Custine retreated from the Rhine.

But the common danger did not hold the Convention together. To encourage recruitment it had been decided to send eighty-two deputies, as *représentants en mission*, into the Departments. The Girondins voted that Jacobins should go, hoping to weaken them – instead it enabled them to strengthen provincial Jacobin Clubs in certain towns. Then the Girondins tried to implicate Danton in Dumouriez's treason. This drew a crushing denunciation upon them and lost them the support of the Plain: Dumouriez had been too long their general for them not to bear some of the odium for his desertion. They were determined, now, to defeat the Jacobins to save themselves and in April had Marat arraigned before the Revolutionary Tribunal. It was a mistake: he was acquitted amid acclamation and the Jacobins entered into a deliberate alliance with the *sans-culottes*. The result was that Cambon persuaded the Convention to pass the *cours forcé*, making the *assignats* the sole legal tender and punishing those who refused to accept them. Then, after much agitation and petitioning, a *Maximum des grains* was declared on 4 May requiring departments to fix grain and fodder prices at the average of prices charged between January and May and to ensure supplies to markets, if necessary by requisitioning: '*Les corps administratifs et municipaux sont également autorisés ... à requérir tout marchand ... d'en apporter aux marchés la quantité nécessaire*'.

But at the very moment when it seemed that the Girondins had been defeated, they counter-attacked in a manner that showed they were worthy opponents for the Jacobins. They endeavoured to 'capture' the Sections by 'infiltration' – precisely the method that had gained them control of Bordeaux and Marseilles and was to gain them Lyons and Toulon. To 'capture' the Sections would mean the collapse of Jacobin hopes of seizing power. It was also necessary to seize control of the Sectional Committees for they were beginning to present petitions for the expulsion of Girondin deputies and to suggest that the rich should equip volunteers at their own expense, as a short of 'super' or additional tax. Something of a class struggle between the *sans-culottes* and the *culottes dorées* developed. In *Le Père Duchesne* Hébert complained that the Sectional Committees were being 'invaded' by the election of a different type of person from normal: the *sans-culottes* were being displaced by *'des visages inconnus ... des banquiers, des marchands de sucre, des bandes de fourriquets aux culottes serrées'*. A further step was taken on 12 May, when the Convention ordered the Sectional Committees to surrender their minute books for examination. An informed observer commented: *'Le parti Jacobin a évidemment manqué son coup'*. On the 15th Gaudet recommended substitute deputies be called to Brouges in case the Convention were attacked, and that day the *Bordelais* arrived from Bordeaux, determined to *'terrasser la faction'*. It was the culmination of the Girondin campaign against the predominance of Paris. Other *fédérés* arrived from the provinces, where the Jacobin Commissioners were sometimes insulted. But not all of those who came were true Girondins, some wanted the overthrow of the Republic – an officer from Gard wrote: 'The two main factions tearing us apart are abominable. Brissot, Pétion and Gaudet are as much to be feared as Marat, Danton or Robespierre'.

Dutard, that ubiquitous police spy, could urge Garat, the Minister of the Interior, *'prenez guarde que les subsistences ne manquent pas à Paris'*, but it was no longer simply a matter of the Maximum. If the Revolution was to survive, Jacobin and *sans-culotte* alike had to take what defensive action they could. Had Garat been a Cromwell the Revolution might have ended here, for the Girondins came near to success; but their rivals were lucky in that the Minister of the Interior was a political trimmer, determined to survive. Dutard accused him of '*quiétisme tou pur*'. On 18 May Barère secured a Commission of Twelve deputies to investigate the behaviour of the Commune. It was composed of Girondins and on the 24th arrested four leading *sans-culottes*. including Varlet and Hébert, the deputy *procureur*. When the Commune protested, Isnard was misguided enough to threaten, in the spirit of the Brunswick Manifesto, 'I declare to you, in the name of the whole of France, that Paris should be annihilated: men would soon be searching the banks of the Seine to see whether Paris had existed'.

At the end of the month, the Jacobins ended the career of the Girondins. On 27 May a crowd invaded the Convention and secured the suppression of the Commission. It was reinstated next day, but the prisoners were released. That evening, following the pattern of 10 August, a central committee was formed at the Hôtel de Ville to direct the coup, probably under Varlet, and Hanriot took over the National Guard. A revolutionary militia of some 20,000 *sans-culottes* at 4 sous a day (a pittance) was raised. Danton and the *Comité de Salut Public* let events take their course.

On 31 May a demonstration to intimidate the Convention was staged and a petition demanding the arrest of twenty-two Girondin deputies was presented. Mme Roland was arrested, but her husband escaped. The Convention merely referred the petition to the Committee of Public Safety, once more suppressing the Commission of Twelve. This first attempt had failed: it was a Friday and men were still at work – and also the Jacobins perhaps feared an outright attack on the Convention by the Sections. But there was no mistake on Sunday, 2 June, a holiday and the best organized coup of the Revolution. It was bloodless, too. Demanding the arrest of Girondin deputies, Hanriot surrounded the Convention. Perhaps hoping to rouse their supporters (the Beaurepaire Section had declared Roland under their protection on 31 May) Hérault de Séchelles, their president, with all the dignity at his command, led a parade of the deputies out of the building proudly asserting their immunity from arrest –

these men who had in April imprisoned Marat, a fellow deputy. Met by Hanriot's unmoving troops, the deputies returned to their seats and meekly voted the arrest of twenty-two Girondin deputies. The insurrection was over: Varlet regretted that there had been no bloodshed.

The Jacobins were the victors of 2 June: their support ensured that the *sans-culottes* would be successful, and not fail as in February and March. But the Jacobins refused to enforce the *enragé* programme. They had won their chance to invigorate national defence and save the Revolution: they could only achieve this end by keeping the support of the provinces as well as the *sans-culottes*. To allow the *enragé* policy of a general maximum, a 'revolutionary army' to gather food supplies, the arrest of all suspects and a purge of all noble officers, would have raised the provinces against them. They had also to preserve the Convention – 'for the dictatorship of the *Montagnards*', as Lefebvre puts it. Except that they could hope for greater sympathy from the Jacobins, the *sans-culottes* had come out of the crisis empty-handed, having taken all the risks, (see D. Guérin, *La lutte des classes sous la première République*, 2 vols, Paris, 1946). The Jacobins suppressed the insurrectionary committee on 8 June. But the economic problems remained: it would take a still greater foreign threat and a further insurrection to bring the *sans-culottes* within sight of their aims.

The Girondins were merely placed under house arrest. Some were to escape and their followers in the provinces were to raise a real threat of federalism. The Girondins had, apparently, ceased to be revolutionaries, or rather they desired to freeze the Revolution at the point where they were in command and the *sans-culottes* under control. Though things had been in their favour once, they had made almost every possible mistake. Personal jealousies had consumed their objectives; the war they had promoted had not been prosecuted vigorously; all necessary exceptional measures had been opposed in a doctrinaire way, and in the same way they had ignored the very real suffering of the *menu peuple*, to whom they had appeared indifferent. They had begun by denouncing the king and demanding a republic, yet, in the event, they could not bring themselves to give substance to their words. As Michelet put it: '*Ce parti devenait peu à peu l'asile du royalisme; le masque protecteur sous lequel la Contre-Révolution put se maintenir à Paris en presence de la Révolution même*'. The royalist Charles de Lacretelle, who had bitterly opposed them, was writing in their papers in the spring of 1793. Yet, for all their vacillation and the failure that enveloped them, the Girondins have retained a place of honour in the history of the Revolution – this could not have been merely because of their oratory.

PART V
The Fourth Phase: 1793–4

[14] CIVIL WAR, INVASION AND THE TERROR

For over a hundred and fifty years, the Jacobins, who were now to save France, have been portrayed as bloodthirsty terrorists with criminal inclinations. Yet, like the Girondins, they were the men of 10 August 1792, indeed, were to be distinguished from their rivals only in that they were realist enough to compromise their theory in the face of exceptional circumstances. So far were they from seeking blood, that their rivals, the Girondins, were not massacred until the autumn, and only then because of the crisis that had continued to grow throughout the summer. The Jacobin Terror, which features so largely in the popular view of the Revolution, did not properly begin until the autumn of 1793 – four years after the march of the women to Versailles – and the image of the guillotine spouting blood for the enjoyment of the *tricoteuses*, belongs to a few short months.

An impossible situation faced the Jacobin victors in the summer of 1793 – invasion, civil war, and a worsening economic crisis. Their immediate task was to gain peasant support. This would save them from the extravagance of the *enragés*, keep them in power, save France and stop the peasants joining the Federalist Revolt. In the last resort, any government in France depended on the peasant. Consequently, a further step in the land settlement was taken. On 3 June the sale of *émigré* property in small lots, with the Treasury advancing sums for up to ten years, was approved. This was a bad deal for the Treasury, for repayment was made in the rapidly depreciating *assignats*. Many bourgeois benefited from the easy terms, but so did some peasants and it created a powerful interest in the survival of the Revolution (and the Jacobins) in order to retain the land. Furthermore, it prevented a wholesale seizure of property arising out of land-hunger and the pressures of an increased population: in this sense it was '*une grande mesure conservatrice*' that both preserved and limited the Revolution. On 6 June villages were empowered to lease an *arpent* (*c.* 1½ acres) of land to families owning less than one, and to divide common land if they wished. On 17 July came the final destruction of feudalism by the abolition of any charge whatever arising out of feudal law. The fall of the Girondins brought conspicuous benefits to the peasant proprietors, and they remained the socially conservative opponents of capitalist methods in agriculture (see page 32), entrenched in power until the radical changes after 1945. Napoleon was at pains to guarantee their position: they stood by their land and the defeat of the privilege of the Ancien Régime. Like the bourgeoisie, they too were victors in the Revolution, yet they have been too often overlooked.

Further support for the Jacobins was gained by the Constitution of 1793, drafted by Hérault de Séchelles, presented in June and approved by a plebiscite. Fears of a dictatorship of Paris were dispelled by granting universal male suffrage and a referendum; furthermore, property was writ large in the Declaration of Rights that prefaced the Constitution – '*La sûreté consiste dans la protection accordée par la société à chacun de ses membres pour la conservation de sa personne, de ses droits et de ses propriétés ... Nul ne peut être privé de la moindre portion de sa propriété sans son consentement*'. There was to be no nonsense about the *loi agraire*; but social democracy was not forgotten, for the guarantee of rights included '*une instruction commune*' and '*des secours publics*'. Approved by 1,800,000 votes, it was never enforced because of the crisis, but reverently placed in a casket in the middle of the Convention: '*cette crèche fut son tombeau*' commented Barère. The Terror made this certain.

These changes helped the Jacobins to defeat the Federal

Revolt, a real civil war that went far towards destroying not merely '*la République une et indivisible*' but France herself. Many factors lay behind the revolt – local particularism, fear for property, *Feuillant* opposition to democracy, the influence of refractory priests and royalists, but also the activities of local Girondins and those deputies who had escaped from Paris. Fortunately the frontier departments, perhaps because of the behaviour of the allies and *émigrés*, remained loyal, but some sixty departments were in more or less open revolt. There was talk of seeking English help, Bordeaux wrote to General Custine calling on him to rally to the Girondist cause, and the Midi asserted an independence of Paris that might be thought to foreshadow 1870 or 1940. But there was little cooperation between departments and the Girondins did not seek help from foreigners or join the Vendéans. On the whole the peasants did not join the rebels and the Jacobins were able to defeat them severally – in Brittany and Normandy by July, but it was October before Bordeaux was recaptured, Tallien executing some three hundred. The revolt was most serious in the south, and it is strange that it should be almost forgotten in the story of the Revolution.

Nîmes and Toulouse, perilously near the Spanish frontier, were in revolt, but the real civil war, fought with a savagery almost equal to that in the Vendée, was centred on Lyons, Marseilles and Toulon. The army in the Alps was cut off and the rebels openly appealed to foreigners. In August Toulon proclaimed 'Louis XVII' and admitted Admiral Hood and the English fleet – a disaster worse than Trafalgar for this meant the loss from the Mediterranean naval base of 26 out of the 65 ships of the line, all in good order. The Jacobins did not recapture the city until December, helped by the artillery of the young Bonaparte: small wonder that Barras shot several hundred rebels there. Marseilles had been recaptured in August, just in time to prevent its surrender to the British. Lyons presented the most serious threat: in July the local Jacobin leader Chalier was beheaded and the *émigré* Comte de Précy took command. Fearing that Piedmont would send help, Kellerman began a siege that lasted from August to October, absorbing badly needed troops and both pre-

venting the speedy recapture of Toulon and isolating the army
in the Alps. Repression followed. Lyons was proclaimed '*une
ville affranchie*' and the homes of the rich were to be demolished.
Couthon proved too mild a repressor and was replaced by Collot
d'Herbois and Fouché, whose *mitraillades* took a fearsome toll of
rebel lives.

By the Autumn the Federal Revolt was over, and most of the
Girondins were dead. Twenty-one of those remaining in Paris
were executed in October following Amar's Report on their
activities. Those who escaped from Paris were hunted down in
the provinces, Barbaroux shot himself, but was still alive when
guillotined; Pétion and Buzot shot themselves and their bodies
were found in the fields, mauled by dogs; Roland, hearing of his
wife's execution, committed suicide at Rouen. There had been
such an admixture of royalism in the Revolt that the recurrent
idea of a plot to overthrow the Revolution seemed to be coming
true; the British blockade and the activities of Pitt's spies,
together with several serious fires in government arsenals added
weight to the idea – Pitt was declared 'an enemy of the human
race'. The rich were suspected and it was more than ever necessary to purge the clubs and administrative bodies of 'unreliable'
patriots – an essential ingredient of the Terror. And at the
height of the Revolt, on 13 July, Marat was stabbed in his bath
by Charlotte Corday.

She came from Normandy, but was not, it seems, a Girondin
agent. A most effective assassin – she had pinned her baptismal
certificate and an *adresse aux Français* to her dress to explain
her deed, lest she be lynched – she has taken a place among the
heroines of France. But, if her purpose had been to avenge the
death of Louis XVI, she had waited six months and, if it were to
avert the coming Terror or to overthrow the Jacobins, she had
chosen the wrong victim. For Marat had been the safety valve
of the Jacobins: his violent language gained them *sans-culotte*
support while saving them from too close a dependence on men
like Hébert and Jacques Roux. His murder weakened them and
brought the Terror nearer. There was a furious outcry and
'*l'ami du peuple*' was exhibited to the public, wound and all, a

Jacobin Martyr. He was given a public funeral and his heart suspended from the ceiling of the Cordelier Club.

We will never know the real Marat, for counter-revolutionaries have consistently cast him for the rôle of the basest of terrorists, blaming him for the September Massacres, if not for the Terror of the autumn of 1793 (though he died in July). His career was unusual and chequered, but his enemies refuse him a place as a scientist and doctor, calling him a charlatan and a quack, even ridiculing employment as doctor to the Comte d'Artois's guard at 2,000 livres a year. It seems almost that his skin complaint, that obliged him to seek relief in baths, is regarded as a sign of divine displeasure. With the coming of the Revolution he had given up everything for politics and throughout he was a lone wolf always crying 'nous sommes trahis'. He was persecuted because of the violence of his newspapers – contracting his skin disease when hiding in cellars and sewers – but the menu peuple knew him for their friend. If his language was violent, he was not lacking in idealism, and, as Soboul puts it, he was always conscious of the realities of the political struggle. True, he respected property as little as persons, and this may have been enough to condemn him in many eyes. But his death inspired a curious cult to his memory. Two months after the Thermidor crisis, on the second anniversary of the Republic, on 21 September 1794, his ashes were placed in the Panthéon (to be cast out again in February 1795). David's fine pietà, 'Homage à Marat', despite its romanticism, may be nearer to the real Marat than the violent language of many historians.

In the Vendée, too, the Revolution continued to face a serious menace. In July the rebels threatened Angers and the Convention ordered the Vendée to be devastated, though the rebels remained victorious. But by the autumn they were beginning to lose ground and in December Marceau replaced the sans-culotte generals to defeat the rebels, although guerrilla warfare continued intermittently. A Commission de recensement at Angers executed two thousand rebels and military courts shot many more. The prisons were so full at Nantes that fear of a break-out led to the noyades which Carrier did nothing to stop. Probably three thousand died in December and January. The Vendée was not utterly vanquished, but the danger was greatly reduced.

Throughout the crisis of the summer hostile armies had been pressing on each frontier. Why had France not been crushed by the First Coalition, which Pitt formed and financed for this very purpose? The courts of Europe hated the Revolution, and the web of myths that was to present it as the harbinger of barbarism and the Jacobins as ogres was already being spun among them. But they feared revolution at home if too many troops were sent to fight or too great a strain were put on their people – as Mallet du Pan put it, 'They feared their subjects almost as much as they feared the enemy'. They also lacked great generals. But their principal fault was a failure to recognize the totally novel form of warfare that France developed. By the autumn they were faced with a nation in arms driving a war effort that could be met only by adopting similar methods – which they feared to do. Furthermore, they were confident of an easy victory over a France disorganized, defeated, and, in the phrase of Michelet, stabbed in the back by the Vendéans and federalists. But there was neither common policy nor strategy among them: so France tackled them individually. Pitt must bear much blame for this. Frederick William personally set out for Poland in September: Pitt sent a much needed army to waste in the West Indies in November. A reinvigorated France faced her enemies because they had failed to crush her in the summer of 1793.

There was no denying the invasion threat of that summer. Danton, still in the Committee of Public Safety, could make patriotic speeches – '*que nous vouons tous à la mort ou que nous anéantions les tyrans*' – but the spirit of the previous September seemed to have evaporated in him and secretly he sought peace. But peace when defeated could be purchased only at the price of surrender – the loss of the Revolution, and almost certainly a bitter restoration. Perhaps fear of such capitulation lay behind the clause of the 1793 Constitution, '*Il ne fait point la paix avec un ennemi qui occupe son territoire*'. Danton's replacement on the Committee of Public Safety was no surprise.

War production had slumped and as the military situation

worsened, the generals were suspected (Dumouriez's treason was but two months before); Custine was recalled, later to be guillotined. In the north and east 200,000 Austrians, Prussians, British and allied troops massed on the frontiers. In July Coburg took Condé and Valenciennes, and Mainz fell to the Prussians. Once more the road to Paris lay open. Paris replied with the *Levée en masse* (see page 142). But once more the allies hesitated, divided their forces and wasted time on sieges like the Duke of York at Dunkerque. In the Alps some 25,000 Piedmontese and Neapolitans financed by Pitt, threatened to aid Toulon and Lyons. In September the Spanish invested Perpignan. September was the height of the foreign peril. The inadequacy and disunity of her enemies saved France; but she was vastly helped by the courage and exertions of her people and her Jacobin leaders who were not afraid to apply those emergency measures that are the real meaning of the Terror. But the Terror is no simple phenomenon; it has many aspects and reflected many different circumstances.

Taine, in his great polemic, stressed the fear of plots, the '*thèse du complot*', as the foundation of the Terror: Aulard stressed the foreign crisis and the civil war, the '*thèse des circonstances*'. Both laid insufficient emphasis upon the social aspects, the possible, if unrecognized, emergence of social democracy – for much of the legislation of the Terror was economic. Mathiez, indeed, sees it as a deliberate attempt to produce something like the prototype of a twentieth century totalitarian state centred on Paris. But, in the last resort, it was the country that supported the Terror, not simply Paris. It was, as Lefebvre has argued, another example, upon a vast scale, of the defensive reaction in support of the Revolution that contributed to the Revolutionary Mentality: but it was highly organized – the anarchy of the September Massacres has no place in the Terror of the Year Two.

Paris was the central motor of the Terror; consequently the position of the *sans-culottes* was vital. As we discovered, the Jacobins had refused the *enragé* programme in June but, so long as the Revolution was threatened and its survival rested to some extent upon the Sections, that programme could not be ignored. Conditions worsened as the crisis worsened: September was a desperate month. The *assignat*, down to 36 per cent of its original value in June, had fallen to 22 per cent in August; wages of skilled journeymen had doubled since 1789, but prices still outpaced them, and during the summer they rose at a terrifying rate. Wine, the equivalent of 10/– a litre in 1790, was 16/– in June 1793, and 20/– in September; butter, 12/– a pound in 1790, was 26/– in June, 35/– in September; sugar had risen from 24/– in 1790 to 110/– and soap from 12/– to 70/– (Rudé). Yet this rise in the cost of living was not the whole story, for uncertain market conditions meant sudden fluctuations in prices that led to spontaneous outbursts of anger and '*taxation populaire*', as in March 1793. Shopkeepers were suspected of hoarding and being 'foreign agents' – '*on sait que cette classe en masse est la seule qui ait profité de la Révolution*', police agents reported the popular opinion. Small wonder that there were soap riots in June, when it was forcibly sold at 20 sous a pound. This was the shadow of the *loi agraire* again, and the Jacobins retaliated by attacking Jacques Roux as the instigator of the riots. Marat and Robespierre denounced his methods and he was expelled from the Cordeliers Club: his eclipse and the murder of Marat meant that Hébert led the *sans-culottes* in September. The Hébertists wanted not only economic controls, but sterner measures against 'aristocrats' and a purge of the army command: 'if revolutions are protracted, it is because none but half measures are taken'.

Concessions were made in the summer. In June the Stock Exchange was closed and in July, in a vain attempt to avoid the General Maximum that the *sans-culottes* demanded, the Convention decreed the death sentence for hoarding food and supplies, with a reward for those denouncing the hoarders – an opportunity for individuals to play off old scores that must have led to many inaccurate accusations.

Civil war had disrupted food supplies, especially from Normandy and, though the harvest was good, disorder, drought and lack of wind, as in 1789, stopped the Paris mills so that flour was in very short supply, and dangerous queues formed at bakers. The

news of the surrender of Toulon precipitated a *journée* that was
the culmination of the distress and uncertainty of the summer.
After an uncertain start, Chaumette and Hébert, with the support of the Paris Commune, took control and on 5 September
surrounded the Convention demanding more vigorous action
against 'suspects' by which term they meant not merely potential
counter-revolutionaries, but really their political opponents. It
was really an attempted Hébertist coup. 'No more quarter, no
more mercy for traitors ... The day of justice and wrath has
arrived', declared Chaumette.

If the independence of the Convention and the Committee of
Public Safety was to be preserved, immediate concessions, perhaps the full *sans-culotte* demands of June, were necessary. To
quieten the *sans-culottes*, Billaud-Varenne and Collot d'Herbois
were elected to the Committee and 'Terror' was made 'the order
of the day'. The Revolutionary Tribunal was divided into four
courts sitting concurrently to speed up its work. The long delayed *armée révolutionnaire* was begun on 9 September under
Ronsin, composed of *sans-culottes* and designed to ensure grain
and meat supplies in Paris and maintain order (it was copied in
some provincial cities). But it was not all concessions. Roux and
Varlet were arrested, and Danton had Section meetings reduced
to two a week – a shrewd move that reduced the Sections' powers
and was a step towards the Law of Frimaire (see page 139).
Needy *sans-culottes* were to be compensated by the payment of
40 sous an attendance – an arrangement that caused some resentment amongst them, and some refused the payment for they
would not be called '40-sous patriots'. The payment was abolished
the following August because of its inconveniences. On 17 September came the Law of Suspects, defining them so generally that
the local *comités de surveillance* in effect had a free hand – '*ce
qui ... se sont montrés partisans de la tyrannie, du fédéralisme,
et ennemis de la liberté*'. In fact the law merely legalized powers
the committees had already assumed, exemplified by the issue
of '*certificats de civisme*' and '*cartes civiques*'. So much concession
to the Hébertist programme preserved the government, but did
not relieve the food problem. The Convention finally yielded by

passing on 29 September the famous Law of the General Maximum, fixing prices on a great range of essential goods at a third above 1790 levels, but also – to the surprise of the *sans-culottes* – fixing wages at 50 per cent above 1790. This latter point was to have great significance in the future (see page 164) but it was forgotten in the enthusiasm of the moment. The Maximum was the great hope of the *sans-culottes*, which they received '*avec transport*', to them it meant the recognition in 'a juridical form of the right to live' (Lefebvre). Unwillingly the Convention had accepted a policy of general economic control as a temporary war measure to harness the full resources of the nation – and to save the *assignat* from utterly collapsing. The state became the motive force behind much of the economic life of the country, especially agriculture and manufacturing war industries: on 22 October, a *Comité de Subsistences* was established to supervise the requisitioning and distribution of food throughout the country and in November, Lindet was put in charge of it. To ensure a vigorous administration, state power became fully coercive; and the people remained faithful to the Revolution.

Thus the Terror was launched. Many factors come together in it: fear of plots, hence the exaggerated fear of 'suspects'; the need for effective administration and for securing food and other supplies and maintaining the economy, hence the exceptional measures; the need to throw back the invader and defeat rebels, hence the conscription of manpower and requisitioning of supplies; the need to protect the state against speculators and defaulting contractors, and the people against food hoarders, and to preserve the morale on the 'home front', hence the guillotine and the dependence on the popular societies. '*La République n'est qu'une grande ville assiègée*' said Barère: but the legislation and administration of the Terror adds up not to the exceptional measures a town takes when besieged, but to what we recognize today as totalitarian government on a national scale, in a country that could not be certain of loyalty everywhere, without a civil service trained in complex administrative techniques or railways to speed administration, bankrupt after six years of crisis and eighteen months of disastrous foreign war. During the ten months or so of the Terror, in a hand-to-mouth way, the Jacobin leaders saved France and the Revolution and, unintentionally no doubt, pointed the way of the future. The details of how France survived, however, have too often been washed away in the blood of the guillotine, which has too easily become the melodramatic symbol of the Terror.

[15] THE DIFFERENT ASPECTS OF THE TERROR

The steps to revolutionary government

The Terror was not consciously planned: the Jacobins had neither the experience of a comparable revolution to guide them, nor a Lenin to theorize and plan their actions. All they had was determination in the face of the crisis that had developed. Vigorous action was needed to concentrate the full residuary powers of the State in defence of the Revolution, both at home and abroad. At the same time they had to preserve themselves in power by steering an uneasy course between the Right Wing of the Convention and the Left Wing of the *sans-culottes*. Sieyès had already justified revolutionary government in 1789: 'the nation exists before everything and it is the origin of everything, its wish is always legal and it is a law unto itself'. Robespierre, who became the apologist for the Terror, enlarged this Rousseauesque principle by giving a moral basis of civic virtue to revolutionary dictatorship: '*Le jour où le pouvoir tombera dans des mains impures et perfides, la liberté sera perdue, son nom deviendra le prétexte et l'excuse de la contre-révolution même, son énergie sera celle d'un poison violent*'. As the Terror progressed, it was to develop the theory that lies at the base of any dictatorship by a minority, and to become something of a vehicle for the promotion of civic virtue – for, with Robespierre, one catches a glimpse of the crown of Savonarola, if not of Calvin. But, in the

Autumn of 1793, this was lost in the future. When they accepted
the logic of the Terror, the Jacobins were not dreaming of a
theocracy.

The suspension of the king after Varennes (see page 75) had
created a precedent for the Assembly assuming executive powers,
and local *comités de surveillance* had then been spontaneously
organized to watch 'suspects'. Thereafter, the steps to revolutionary government were gradual and to some extent simply
accidental. In the crisis of the first invasion and the fall of the
throne, the Girondins, so keen for decentralization, had been
compelled to appoint the Executive Council of Ministers, in
which Danton had predominated, and to take emergency measures (see page 106). Though these were gradually withdrawn, the
king's execution and the second invasion had created a similar
crisis by April 1793, which was to culminate in the autumn. In
January 1793 a large, unwieldy *Comité de Sûreté Générale*, composed of minor provincial politicians now on the fringe of national
politics, men like Amar and Vadier, was elected to supervise the
prisons and police work – it was a committee that was not
insignificant: it played a vital rôle in the Thermidor crisis (see
page 165). In March 1793 Danton had an extraordinary Revolutionary Tribunal established to avoid another September
Massacre – 'Let us be terrible in order to prevent the people
being terrible'. Then in April, to meet the national crisis, came
the First (Dantonist) *Comité de Salut Public* (see page 118).
Isnard even proposed that it should take over the Council of
Ministers. The Convention, however, retained ultimate control
by having the right every month to re-elect its members who
were drawn from the Convention.

The fall of the Girondins saw no change of policy, merely a
more vigorous government. Discredited by the failure of the war
effort, and perhaps, also, by General Dillon's plot to save the
queen and Louis XVII, Danton was replaced on the Committee. Indeed, on 10 July virtually a new Committee was
elected: Barère, who maintained liaison with the Convention,
Lindet, who, despite his dislike of terrorism, became in effect
minister of the interior, Hérault de Séchelles, perhaps for diplo-

macy, Jeanbon Saint-André, often on mission to the navy, Prieur de la Marne, often on mission to the army, Saint-Just, also often away, and Couthon. The latter two were resolute Jacobins who had often to rally their more moderate colleagues. Robespierre did not join the committee until 27 July (apparently on Couthon's suggestion) – he became its spokesman in both the Convention and the Jacobin Club. The conservative engineers, Carnot and Prieur de la Côte d'Or, were elected on 14 August to strengthen the military machine, and the Great Committee of the Year Two, was completed by the election of Billaud-Varenne and Collot d'Herbois on 6 September as a concession to the Hébertists. From the beginning there was lack of agreement and personal antipathy among them, but they held together because of the national emergency: 'The Terror was a dictatorship of distress', as Carnot's son put it. They divided the tasks of government among themselves, meeting in the mornings to divide the work and reporting every evening. No minutes were kept and there was no formal method of taking decisions, nor any apparent evidence of collective responsibility. Fortunately they were all fairly young men, for the pace of work was killing – twelve hours a day and no holidays: they were under a very great strain. Furthermore, they had to fight to preserve their power both against the excesses of the Hébertists and the intrigues of discontented members of the Convention. In the midst of the September crisis there was a move in the Convention to attack the economic controls: it was Robespierre who defeated it – 'In two years 100,000 men have been butchered because of treason and weakness. It is weakness for traitors that is destroying us'. For the moment the Convention retired into second place, allowing the Committee to become the government of France. But the Convention should not be forgotten or thought merely subservient: it was the Convention that won in Thermidor.

The Committee gradually centralized administration to produce the totalitarian government that made France victorious. Conscription in August; requisitioning and price controls in September; the Convention's declaration on Saint-Just's report of 10 October, '*Le gouvernement provisoire de la France sera révolutionnaire jusqu'à la paix*', merely recognized a fact. The Convention's principles had not been abandoned, but deferred during the crisis: constitutional government meant the separation of powers, decentralization, the rule of law with an independent judiciary, while the characteristics of revolutionary government were quite the opposite – '*Toute mesure de sûreté doit être prise par le conseil exécutif provisoire, sous l'autorisation du comité [de salut public]*', and the suppression of the rule of law by summary tribunals untrammelled by normal judicial procedure. Before its reorganization (see page 133) the Revolutionary Tribunal had condemned only some 26 per cent of those who came before it: after September, the long line of political victims grew in volume. In October the queen, with becoming dignity, ended a career that had done so much to destroy the monarchy, then twenty-one Girondon deputies followed her (Valazé being guillotined although he had already stabbed himself), then Barnave, the unworthy Philippe Égalité (once Duc d'Orléans), and Bailly, whose execution recalled the massacre of the Champ de Mars and added a class feeling. The executions were to continue, though the victims were not even predominantly 'aristocrats'. But it was not until December that the Committee had established, at least on paper, effective central control by the great Law of Frimaire (see page 139). Even then it needed the guillotine to ensure unity; as Robespierre declared, '*Il faut une volonté une*'.

The restoration of central control

A less obvious, but nonetheless important, effect of the Federalist Revolt was the virtual breakdown of local administration in many areas. To ensure the 'unity of the Republic' and the enforcing of government decrees, a purge of local committees and a vigilant watch on their activities was necessary. Saint-Just had complained of civil servants supplying the Vendéans with flour, and speculating in food was a commonplace: the Maximum would encourage such speculation – hence the need for vigilance at a local level. This vigilance was supplied by local Jacobin clubs, especially as requisitioning of supplies and horses developed in the autumn. This frequently meant that Jacobins became civil servants, sometimes positions being created for them – at Metz, 61 out of the 148 members of the Jacobin Club there held some government office. Many were to suffer for their exertions after Thermidor.

To ensure compliance with central government decrees, *Représentants en Mission,* were sent off by the Convention, like the eighty-two commissioners sent in March to help raise the levy of 300,000 men. They were sent both to the armies to maintain morale and ensure the loyalty of generals and to local areas to encourage and supervise local committees. They were a useful way of delegating authority and became, until December, the eyes and ears of the *Comité de Salut Public.* Their orders were treated as *lois provisoires,* and in the chaos of the summer they acted independently – speed was necessary, there was no time to await orders from Paris. In many ways they assumed much the positions of the old intendants (see page 34), except that they had greater initiative. They varied in quality, some limiting their functions, others being very vigorous, purging local committees and supervising civil servants and contractors. Some were excellent, like Lakanal, others were cruel, if effective, like Fouché at Lyons or Carrier at Nantes. Their vigour exaggerated the effect of the Terror in certain places: it was bloody only in exceptional areas. Their contribution to the survival of the Republic is not to be overlooked: until the spring of 1794, only fear of the *Comité de Salut Public* held them in check.

The last large-scale mission of deputies to the provinces was to enforce the great Law of Frimaire in December 1793. The *Comité de Salut Public* lacked the time and the resources to push centralization of authority to its logical conclusion (if, indeed, it wished to do so), but with so many bodies wielding local initiative – especially the local *armées révolutionnaires* – it was essential to enforce a unified policy in order to avoid chaos. The Law of 14 Frimaire (4 December) was passed for this reason: as Mathiez says, 'with a few alterations, [it] was to be the provisional Constitution of the Republic for the duration of the war'.

Administrative centralization had returned, but in a form far more effective than it had ever been under the Bourbons. The *Comité de Salut Public* controlled all local officials and unreliable ones were purged. National agents, *'spécialement chargés de requérir et de poursuivre l'exécution des lois'* had to write a report every ten days to both the *Comité de Salut Public* and the *Comité de Sûreté Générale*. The volume of paperwork is well illustrated by a diagram in J. M. Thompson's *The French Revolution* (p. 377), although he omits to note the Convention. Departmental authorities were strictly confined to local functions and to obeying instructions and, foreshadowing the *préfets* of Napoleon, the officials had to be approved and appointed by the *Comité de Salut Public*. Severe penalties awaited officials who failed in their duty.

By this means the Jacobin leaders re-established the administrative unity of the Republic, and their methods have been copied by almost every totalitarian state and those states faced by a great crisis – like England in the two World Wars. But they were not looking to the future, they were acting for survival in self-defence. On 25 December a circular justifying the new law was somewhat apologetic, blaming earlier de-centralization for promoting *'les principes de fédéralisme'*; and acknowledging that revolutionary government was of a provisional nature only, for the duration of the war: *'Ce n'est pas assez d'avoir trouvé le topique, il faut l'appliquer sur-le-champ. . . . L'intensité révolutionnaire ne peut s'exercer que dans un libre espace, voilà pourquoi le législateur écarte sur la route tout ce qui n'est point guide, tout ce qui est obstacle'*.

The dechristianizing campaign

The Church had suffered a direct attack in the early years of the Revolution and it had become closely associated with counter-revolution. Furthermore, especially in the towns, a definite cult of 'civic religion', stemming perhaps from indifference to christianity and from anticlericalism, was appearing, borrowing its manners from the church – Le Peletier, Marat and Chalier were venerated as martyrs, and the secular festivals of the Revolution (14 July, 10 August) emulated in some ways the feasts of the church. Debaptism, the naming of children, and adults, after revolutionary heroes and the changing of street names were common features. During the autumn of 1793 anticlericalism rose to a pitch that could only be described as a positive 'dechristianizing' campaign. At Nevers, Chaumette and Fouché, as *représentants en mission*, had in September stripped the church of its treasures for the war effort, unveiled a bust of Brutus in the church and ordered burial in a common cemetery, with 'death is an eternal sleep' inscribed over the gateway. A similar movement in Paris was of greater consequence, since it was copied in other towns. Dechristianizing was popular with the *sans-culottes*, and it was suspected that Hébert might be behind the whole campaign, for political ends. But it was supported by others than the Hébertists.

It was on Fabre d'Eglantine's recommendation that the Revolutionary Calendar was adopted in October, taking 22 September 1792, the first day of the Republic, as its origin. The calendar was dechristianized, saints' days disappeared and Sundays were replaced by *décadi* – an unpopular move since it gave a holiday every ten instead of seven days. The year was divided into twelve equal months of thirty days, with five extra days called '*sans-culottides*', and in November picturesque, appropriate names were given to the months, like Thermidor, Vendémiaire and Brumaire (see Appendix III). For the rest of the century, important events are known by these unusual names. The English, however, were not impressed and translated them as Wheezy, Sneezy, Freezy; Slippy, Drippy, Nippy; Showery, Flowery, Bowery; Wheaty, Heaty, Sweety.

In November the Convention attended a great Festival of Reason, celebrated in Notre-Dame itself, with a mountain constructed in the choir and an actress impersonating Liberty. Then the Paris Commune closed all churches not taken over by the new cult of Reason, an action widely copied throughout France. Priests continued to practise, even in Paris, but they were well aware of their danger. But the attack on religion was a mistake, for it did not promote unity. Robespierre suspected atheism lurked behind the campaign, and the fear grew that it was associated with the 'Pitt plot' to overthrow the Revolution from within by encouraging extreme and disruptive policies. As early as October, Fabre d'Eglantine denounced the leaders of the campaign (see page 153). Curiously enough, it was this very action that was to lead to the destruction of both the Hébertists and the Dantonists in the complex crisis of Germinal, Year Two.

The problem of supplies in the controlled economy

The summer crisis led to many emergency decrees; grain requisitioning began in August and price controls were placed on all types of fuels and oats. On 23 August came the *Levée en masse,* the attempt to conscript the whole active population for the war effort; this was a people's war. The decree resulted from 'iron' Carnot, called 'the organizer of victory', joining the *Comité de Salut Public,* with Prieur de la Côte d'Or, who organized equipment, arms and ammunition. Lindet was later to organize food, clothing and military transport. From the point of view of logistics, all three should share Carnot's title. The decree mobilized unmarried men aged 18 to 25 for the armies, married men for military transports and munition factories, women for making tents and uniforms and service in hospitals, children to make bandages and old men to be carried to the public square '*pour exciter le courage des guerriers, la hain des rois et l'unité de la République*'. This decree launched modern totalitarian warfare: '*Dès ce moment, jusqu'à celui où les ennemis auront été chassés du territoire de la République, tous les Français sont en réquisition permanente pour la service des armées*'.

General requisitioning was bound to follow the decree, for the problem would be how to feed, clothe and equip the vast army that would result – most of the arms factories were within reach of the enemy and Saint-Étienne was in rebel hands, while the British blockade stopped the import of steel, salt-petre, potash and sulphur. Time was precious, the danger was great: since private contractors could not guarantee supplies, the *Comité de*

Salut Public had to regulate production. Regardless of politics, industrialists like Périer and Chaptal, a federalist, bankers like Perregaux, a foreigner in touch with Pitt, and scientists were called upon – Hassenfratz, a distinguished chemist and mining engineer was engaged on increasing arms manufacture in Paris, helped by Monge, the mathematician, Fourcroy, and others; Berthollet the chemist experimented with explosive shells at Meudon, and with the balloon later used at Fleurus – it was a pity that Lavoisier, France's greatest scientist of the age, had to die as a former farmer-general. Munition workers were exempt from conscription, like the transport workers, but were under semi-military discipline and liable to arrest as 'suspects' if they struck. Transport proved a problem, for horses and carts had to be requisitioned without harming agriculture. But all business was put at the disposal of *la patrie en danger* – to ensure enough leather for harnesses, butchers had to hand over skins and tanners to keep their bark pits full; shoemakers had to produce two pairs of boots per journeyman per *décade*. Brass and metal from church bells were commandeered – and table linen too; and at Strasbourg Saint-Just, on mission, exacted 20,000 pairs of shoes. New state factories for armaments and munitions were opened, and existing factories given production targets and encouraged to adopt new processes recommended by the scientists. By 1794 some 5,000 metal workers were employed in Paris, some working in the Tuileries gardens, eventually producing 700 muskets a day, while the provinces produced only 600 – Paris was truly the arsenal of France, for in addition it produced 12,000 sabres and bayonets and her four new gun foundries turned out 1,500 cannon a year. Since the shortage of saltpetre endangered the supply of gun powder, Prieur de la Côte d'Or created a national organization for its production, with 28 refineries, and workers being brought to Paris to be trained – by 1794 some 200 tons had been produced from scraping cellar walls and from sewers. Chappe established semaphore telegraph from Lille to Paris to speed information – the Admiralty copied the idea from Portsmouth to Whitehall.

This industrial mobilization was a remarkable anticipation of twentieth-century conditions of total war. Well might Europe stand amazed. Remember that the Jacobins had no experience to lean on: vital supplies were often held up, even for the army, and the population was predominantly agricultural, with few trained workers, the majority being strangers to industrial processes. In such conditions, to produce overnight synchronized national production was a triumph of organization and determination that can have few equals in history. This background to the dramatic political events has too long been ignored by historians who dismiss the period merely as one of bloodshed and struggles for power. Of course coercion was essential: until the spring, this, with fear for the future of the Revolution, is the real meaning of the Terror: 'Without the Terror, which compelled even the most indifferent to expend *some* effort, the Committee [of Public Safety] would never have been able to restrain the spirit of speculation or to overcome passive resistance' (Lefebvre).

There was the problem of food supply in the towns, too – the more important as much of the energy of revolutionary government came from the *sans-culottes*. They wanted price control and requisitioning because they had to eat. There were a few writers who urged the social ownership of property and the means of production, but Babeuf, the most important, was in jail, and the death penalty was still in force against advocates of the *loi agraire*. The Jacobins were prepared for emergency measures because of the crisis, not for overturning the economic structure of society. The Constitutions of 1791 and 1793 both guaranteed property, and the Jacobins knew that peace would bring a 're-turn to normalcy'. Price control had featured under the Ancien Régime in time of dearth, but the Jacobins were no more willing to introduce it than the Girondins: they would decree the death penalty for hoarders, but even Marat tried to divert attention from the General Maximum. It was the political crisis of September that forced them into controls in order to retain the support of the *sans-culottes* and promote efficient government. The *armée révolutionnaire* had been approved in June: it appeared in Paris only in September, composed of *sans-culottes* but with few wage earners (it was used to suppress movements for higher wages) and allowed the use of the National Guard's cannon. Similar forces in other towns contained more wage earners. The *Comité de Salut Public* appointed its commanders – like Ronsin. It was never an efficient force and was engaged largely on maintaining food supplies, but the Paris force was used in the siege of Lyons (reducing popular pressure in the capital at the same time). It was also used to replace local forces that had been raised without permission – the Law of Frimaire banned such forces '*sous peine d'être regardés comme rebelles à la loi, et traités comme tels*'. But the Jacobins were always cautious of this force so closely associated with the Hébertists, and it is not to be wondered at that it was disbanded on their fall (see page 156) by Barère, the same man who had proposed its formation in September.

The General Maximum (see page 134) stabilized prices – the *assignat*, 23 per cent in August, had risen to 48 per cent in December – but it proved difficult to work, since so many commodities were involved and there was no trained civil service to run it. Wholesalers and traders welcomed it on food as a guarantee against '*taxation populaire*', but they resented price control of commodities: the peasant objected and concealed his grain. Careful and constant vigilance was needed – Chaumette even threatened the 'nationalizing' of wholesaling and manufacturing. But the Committee resisted such suggestions – and, indeed, were not altogether vigorous against hoarding and black-marketeering. The Maximum obliged the requisitioning of supplies, regularized under Lindet's *Comité des Subsistences;* but it showed small concern for the private consumer – patisseries were a thing of the past, and in November standard war bread, '*pain d'égalité*' appeared. Ration cards appeared in Paris for both bread and meat (though this may have been to reduce the danger of disorder resulting from queues at bakers' shops). There was no question of introducing general rationing throughout France, for not only was the administration lacking, but French agriculture could not guarantee a certain and regular supply of food. Regulation of foodstuffs was left to localities and, despite the vigilance, there was plenty of black-marketeering. The Maximum deepened the division between the Hébertists and Dantonists, for the former wanted to take controls further and attacked the Committee for ineffectiveness on food supply. After both factions had fallen, economic controls were relaxed and inflation returned.

From autumn to spring the prescriptive power of the state lay behind the economic life of the nation, and the Terror – denunciation of suspects, and the use of the guillotine – provided the coercive force. The Jacobins were practical men faced by a desperate situation: they were not theorists: they undertook economic controls and organized a period of 'necessary' dictatorship simply to win the war. To see them as precursors of the Marxists, as Mathiez and Guérin tend to suggest, is to put twentieth-century ideology into eighteenth-century minds. They were not out to redistribute ownership of the means of production. When Saint-Just in October, declared 'You must punish not merely traitors but the indifferent as well; you must punish whoever is passive in the Republic. . . . We must rule by iron those who cannot be ruled by justice', he was saying no more than that government should be 'revolutionary' until the peace. The measures to promote total war should not be confused with a wish to follow a socialist programme – the *sans-culottes* had not yet developed the solidarity of the nineteenth-century proletariat, and the Loi le Chapelier, which the Jacobins made no effort to repeal, went unchallenged. Strikes occurred, but for sound economic reasons arising out of inflation. When Robespierre championed the '*menu peuple*', he did so because he felt they were likely to be more virtuous, being poor, than the rich: it was not a class interest in the Marxist sense. The attack on hoarders and speculators was merely patriotic, and the Maximum looked back to the Ancien Régime, perhaps, rather than to the future, so far as contemporaries were concerned. The legislation of the Terror was for national defence in an emergency: it was not intended to be permanent – Saint-Just himself declared that 'The force of events leads us to a position we had never conceived of'. Even the Laws of Ventôse (see page 155) which seemed to foreshadow a redistribution of property, were passed perhaps largely to gain popular support against the Hébertists. Babeuf, though he claimed Robespierre had a socialist plan, was the first socialist proper of the Revolution, for his views embodied a good deal of nineteenth-century socialist programmes. He is the link between Robespierre and socialism, and his conspiracy was easily suppressed. Unquestionably, the revolutionary government saved the working class from extreme misery, as the deprivations of the Year Three were to show, but it was done for national defence, not in the name of a new political philosophy.

France's new armies and the Revolution's victories

The Seven Years' War (1756–63) was a disaster for French arms. After it, major army reforms were begun by Choiseul and Saint-Germain that gave France one of the best armies in the world. The engineer corps and artillery received particular attention, and it is no surprise to find that many of the marshals of Napoleon were officers and n.c.o.s in these specialist corps that called for a higher degree of technical proficiency than was normal in the armies of the time. The Ségur Ordinance of 1781, that concession to the seigneurial reaction, confining all commissioned ranks to nobles (see page 25), was a retrograde step; but in 1787 a strong Army Council was established, with the radical tactician, Guibert, as Secretary. It was a pity the Revolution overtook its proposed reforms, but the new drill book of 1791, introducing severe discipline, remained in force virtually until 1830. Certainly there was great need of reform, for morale and discipline were bad. There were some 10,000 officers, of whom only 3,500 were actively engaged on military duties; but over half the army budget went on payment of officers' salaries. The senior posts were monopolized by the court nobility; as this blocked promotion prospects, it is no wonder that many junior officers as well as n.c.o.s supported the Revolution. In the ranks there was much ill-feeling, and it had been the salvation of the Third Estate that the Court could not rely on the loyalty of the troops – small wonder, for the officers themselves had given a lead to mutiny by siding with the nobility in the *révolte nobiliaire*, particularly in Brittany in 1787. When the emigration began, the royalists hoped the loss of officers would paralyse the army;

indeed the king actively encouraged emigration (see page 84).
By 1794 some 6,000 officers had emigrated and, though the gaps
left were filled by promoting junior officers and n.c.o.s, eventually producing a far better fighting force, the extent of the disruption and the collapse of morale, was shown clearly in the
disastrous opening of the war when whole battalions deserted,
murdering their officers. But the newly appointed officers had the
confidence of their men: the Revolution guaranteed a career
open to talent, especially for the soldier – by 1794 the generals
were often in their thirties and brought to campaigning a vigour
that was utterly unmatched in the armies of their enemies.

The early volunteers had proved difficult to discipline, though
their quality had been good on the whole; but after Jemappes
many of them simply went home, supposing the war to be over.
As the second invasion threat appeared, more volunteers had to
be raised, often by coercion, like the 300,000 ordered in March
1793. The generals, too, had to be watched carefully: Bouillé
had betrayed the Revolution, and then Lafayette and Dumouriez
deserted to the Austrians. It was not surprising that there
should be continual pressure to purge the high command – especially as Bouchotte, the War Minister, was himself an old soldier with no sympathy with the foibles of an officer class. Defeat
was often regarded as betrayal, thus the fall of Mainz in July
1793 hastened the execution of Custine: several generals were
guillotined for losing a battle – but not all of them; Jourdan was
defeated many times before winning at Fleurus.

The French had the advantage of the best artillery in Europe –
Gribeauval's artillery had won the cannonade at Valmy – but
they also had young men with new ideas well aware of Guibert's
views on tactics that differed so much from the stereotyped
countermarching of eighteenth-century warfare. These ideas,
rather than experience of sniping in America, which in the nature
of things could have been witnessed by only a few soldiers, were
to change military tactics. The need for men meant conscription
and France had a large enough population not to be badly hit
by heavy losses (see page 17). Conscription meant undertrained
troops for whom precision movements were irrelevant. The prac-

tice of forming squares against cavalry charges, which was to save the British at Waterloo, did not reappear in the revolutionary armies until 1795. Speed, the concentration of artillery fire and massed troop movements making full use of the terrain was how the early victories were gained: 'Always manoeuvre *en masse*, and on the offensive . . . use the bayonet on every possible occasion', wrote Carnot in February 1794. It is Carnot, the man behind the great levies of troops, brilliant at making plans, but short-tempered and impatient of generals who showed more caution, who links Guibert with Napoleon.

The *Levée en masse* produced an army of almost a million men by the end of the year, and logistics were a major problem. Prieur de la Côte d'Or saw to the supply of munitions, and Lindet, a forgotten figure, ensured food and other supplies. There were break-downs, but there was much idealism too – civilians wore sabots to save leather and abstained from sugar, wheatbread and other luxuries. There were malingerers and profiteers, too – shoes with paper soles, for instance: the guillotine was a necessary deterrent. The armies were inclined to have a more intelligent rank and file as a result of conscription, but problems of discipline remained, though whole battalions no longer deserted as in 1792. The answer was found in *l'amalgame* (the unification of forces) of February 1793. It was difficult to effect, because of the prejudices of older soldiers against volunteers and conscripts, and was not properly pressed until the spring of 1794 – the regrouping of battalions and the reforming of regiments was easier as heavy losses decimated existing divisions. First the volunteer and conscript levies were amalgamated into a single body, and this was later fused with the regulars, thus ending the confusion of two separate forces. Discipline was restored and morale kept high – *Le Père Duchesne* was distributed free to the armies to maintain the vigour of their republicanism, but they lost the right to petition the Convention as private citizens – 'The armed forces do not deliberate: they obey the laws and execute them', said Carnot. Pensions for the disabled and allowances for widows and orphans were made: 'You must not expect victory from the numbers and discipline of soldiers alone. You

will secure it only through the spread of the republican spirit
within the army', was Saint-Just's opinion.

The situation in the Navy was unhappy. At the beginning of
the Revolution there had been ill-discipline and disorganization
in the fleets, and dockyards. Emigration had a very serious effect,
for the technical knowledge of a deck officer could not easily be
improvised. The loss of so many ships at Toulon was also a serious blow. A dozen years before the French had perhaps out-
classed the British navy in the Maritime War, but it never came
near to this in the Revolution. Difficulties were caused by introducing merchant seamen into the Service, but many of these
turned privateers (Surcouf is a good example) and wrought
havoc on British shipping, despite the naval blockade.

If the Revolution were to be saved, the enemy advancing on
all fronts in the summer of 1793 had to be repulsed. The allied
armies wasted time in unnecessary sieges: the fortresses had to
be held. When the Duke of York besieged Dunkerque, Carnot
wrote: 'it is to be looked at principally from the political point
of view. Above all . . . Dunkerque must be saved, because we
must save the honour of the nation which is involved'. This was
the spirit that Pétain was to invoke to save Verdun in 1916. On
8 September, when Paris was in turmoil, the English and Hano-
verians were beaten at Hondschoote and York retired from
Dunkerque. That month new appointments were made: Jourdan
(aged 31) took command of the *Armée du Nord*, Pichegru (32) of
the *Armée du Rhin* and on 22 October Hoche (25) took over the
Armée de la Moselle. Disorder and confusion was widespread, as
Carnot discovered when he joined Jourdan on mission, but on 16
October, a week after Lyons had been retaken, these two won the
victory that was so badly needed, '*avec un acharnement indicible*'.
The battle of Wattignies was won by the *sans-culottes* levies. The
tide turned slowly and in November Pichegru took the offensive
on the Rhine and Hoche was at Spire in December. The frontier
fortresses were retaken. In the south, the Spaniards were retreat-
ing to the Pyrenees and Kellermann, after retaking Lyons, had
liberated Savoy by October. In December Toulon was retaken,
and Marceau beat the Vendéans at Savenay.

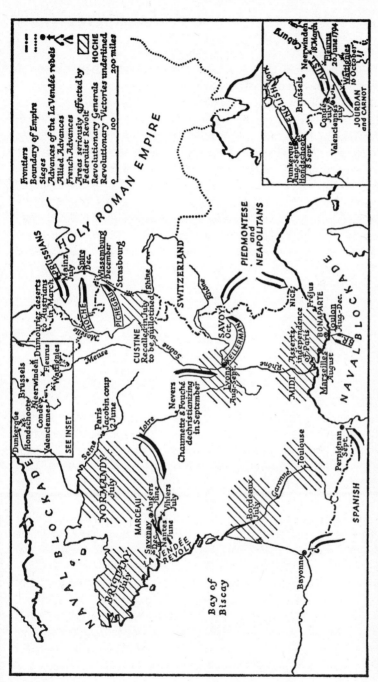

THE SECOND INVASION AND THE FEDERALIST REVOLT, 1793

The disunity of the allies, and the outbreak in the spring, of
the Polish Revolt under Kosciusko, helped to maintain the favourable situation for France. By the new year the military situation
was much relieved and many *Montagnards* wished to moderate
the force of the Terror, especially as prices had remained fairly
stable and the *assignat* had recovered to about 50 per cent. But
the *sans-culottes* were not anxious to see a relaxation of controls,
nor, in this critical stage, when victory was almost achieved,
would a relaxation of effort have been wise. Between the two
forces pulling either to moderate or to maintain the Terror, the
Comité de Salut Public was unenviably placed. Its task was yet
incomplete, for the newly won victories had to be guaranteed:
this was no simple war, no 'sport of kings'. To ensure final victory
it was essential for the Committee to maintain unity.

[16] STRUGGLES FOR POWER

After Wattignies, the moderates began to call for a relaxation of
the Terror; in November, Danton cried 'I ask that the blood of
men be spared'. But to relax the Terror would mean to unwind
the springs of revolutionary government just when they were
being effectively tightened and before the enemy had been properly defeated. Yet to prosecute the Terror more vigorously, as the
Hébertists wanted, would risk wholesale loss of support. Caught
between the cross fire of the two factions, the 'Indulgents' or
Dantonists, and the Hébertists, the Committee came finally to
destroy both in a well conducted coup. Some historians have
seen this as Robespierre playing off the two against each other
in order to become a dictator; but this is to accept uncritically
the picture that the Thermidorians hoped to create. Between
August 1793 and July 1794, the *Comité de Salut Public* lost but
one member: it did not suddenly become Robespierrist. The
Convention which destroyed Robespierre had been seriously
weakened by the loss of the Dantonists. Neither instrument of

government was a compliant tool of Robespierre's; and, when
it is examined, the Robespierrist counter-coup of Germinal
appears rather as a natural reaction to a political threat, than as
a predetermined step to dictatorship. Germinal should not be
compared with the Stalin purges of the 1930s.

Although they were so different, the two factions were curiously linked, first by the 'foreign' or Pitt plot to destroy the Revolution from within by driving it to unnecessary excesses, and which
was to become, in Mathiez's words, 'the canker which was to
consume the Mountain'; and, secondly by the scandal over the
compagnie des Indes, which was to throw suspicion over many
politicians, much as the Panama Scandal was to do a century
later.

It was the excesses of the dechristianizing campaign that began
the moves to the Germinal coup. The campaign varied in intensity in particular areas, but politicians realized that it was making
enemies at home and they feared that the Hébertists were using
it to prepare a new attack on the Convention. Fabre d'Eglantine,
who had fallen out with the extremists, now denounced them as
agents of Pitt and the royalists, and promoters of the 'foreign
plot'. However, one of the dechristianizers was Chabot, a man
suspected of peculation and shortly to be deeply involved in the
compagnie des Indes affair.

During the Revolution, the field for corruption was wide open.
Mirabeau and Danton had sold themselves; but their services to
France were great – this could not be claimed for the men who
now hung around Danton, the '*pourris*' or 'rotters', men who
were simply out to make a fortune. The scandal of the *compagnie
des Indes* was not isolated, it was simply one of the most important because of its political consequences. The company, re-
founded by Calonne, had proved a profitable investment, but in
October 1793 a group of *pourris* conspired to control its liquida-
tion at considerable profit to themselves. Principally, they were
Chabot, Basire, Julien de Toulouse and Fabre d'Eglantine,
assisted by Baron de Batz. When Fabre d'Eglantine denounced
the dechristianizers, the Committees arrested several Hébertists
including Maillard, the hero of the Bastille and the October

(1789) Days, whose vigilance Fabre had reason to fear. Chabot, implicated in the denunciation, retaliated by accusing his accusers of being agents of Batz. With admirable tact, the Committees imprisoned Chabot, Julien and Basire fearing that there might be some connexion, through Chabot, between the 'foreign plot' and the extremists. Further enquiries revealed Fabre's part in the *compagnie des Indes* affair and he was imprisoned in January. But meanwhile, Danton, who had been at Arcis-sur-Aube since October with his new wife, returned to defend Basire and later Fabre, his close friends. This undermined Danton's position and seemed, to the anxious men of the Committees, to link him with the 'plot' and those members of the Convention known to oppose the vigorous prosecution of the Terror.

In November, however, Robespierre had joined Danton in an effort to curb the extremists, even getting Chaumette, of the Paris Commune, to break with the dechristianizers and urging the Convention in December to declare the '*Liberté des Cultes*' establishing freedom of worship. He even helped the Indulgents' campaign for relaxing the Terror by reading, in proof, the first numbers of the *Vieux Cordelier* which his friend Camille Desmoulins produced in December. Active terrorists were recalled, thus Ronsin returned from Lyons, Fréron and Barras from Toulon and Carrier from Nantes. But the Indulgents discredited clemency by claiming it for unworthy men, often, indeed, because they feared themselves to mount the guillotine. When an attempt was made in December to replace the two Hébertist members of the *Comité de Salut Public* by Indulgents, and the *Vieux Cordelier* began to attack revolutionary government, Robespierre wondered whether he had not been made Danton's dupe, and whether the Indulgents' attack on the Hébertists was not a prelude to an attack on the Committee itself.

Collot d'Herbois, one of the threatened members of the Committee, returned from Lyons and boldly defended the action of terrorists there: 'Two months ago, when I left you, you were all thirsting for vengeance upon the infamous conspirators of the city of Lyons'. He enjoyed the confidence of the Committee and Robespierre recovered his central position between the two extremist groups. When Fabre's corruption was exposed he was convinced that fault lay on both sides: 'the internal enemies of the French people are divided into two factions', he said, 'One urges us to weakness, the other to excess. One would turn liberty into a Bacchante, the other into a prostitute'. It seems as though the *Comité de Salut Public*, far from controlling the situation, had almost allowed itself to be pushed into a trap. It had escaped, but the twin dangers remained. That it attacked the Hébertists first was merely because they presented the first threat.

By recovering authority at the expense of the popular societies and Sections, the revolutionary government had made itself less dependent upon the *sans-culottes*. Conditions did not get better for the latter; indeed, by the spring there was a renewed food crisis. Despite the vigilance, the General Maximum could not be effectively enforced and the black market flourished (pork butchers sold only cooked pork to evade controlled prices, for example). By January 1794 controls were being widely evaded, eggs and butter selling at twice the controlled price. The *sans-culottes* blamed the government, and the shopkeepers. The Committee had to decide whether to grant further controls or return to freer commerce to regain the co-operation of merchants. They decided on the latter. '*Il fallait guérir le commerce, et non le tuer*', said Barère. Furthermore, despite the wages maximum, strikes for higher wages, which the Hébertist Commune seemed to connive at, were getting frequent, especially in the armaments factories where the Committee controlled wage rates. When *taxation populaire* broke out in the Paris markets in February, it aggravated the serious crisis arising out of the bitter opposition between Hébertists and Indulgents.

Robespierre was ill in February, and it seemed that the Hébertists were preparing a coup among the Sections. Concessions were necessary and on 22 February, Barère presented a new Maximum. Four days later Saint-Just presented the first of the famous Laws of Ventôse to redistribute the property of guilty 'suspects', of whom the Terror had made a great number, among the poor for the extinction of poverty. It was an appeal for sup-

port in effect against the Hébertists and to consolidate the position of the Committee – *'La Révolution est glacée'*, as Saint-Just
put it. But it may have been something more than this: 'We
must give some land to all', he declared, '... we must have
neither rich nor poor'. In May Barère produced a scheme for
poor relief and medical services. All this might point to the concept of a Welfare State, but the Committee had fallen before it
had time to develop these ideas. In any case a vast civil service
was needed even to effect the Laws of Ventôse, and work upon
them tended to aggravate ill-feeling between the two Committees
(see page 165). Thermidor ended any further work on them. The
laws did not gain much support for the Jacobins, for the *sans-
culottes*, though enthusiastic in principle, were not anxious to
come forward; furthermore, owners of property feared the im-
plication of the laws. For all the redistribution of property that
took place during the Revolution, most noble families – even the
émigré ones – were not expropriated: the bourgeoisie did best in
acquiring land, and most peasants still owned insufficient land
to adopt new capitalist methods.

In March, when Ronsin and Hébert talked of insurrection, it
was no surprise that the Hébertists were arrested and charged
with provoking the food shortage for political ends, planning an
insurrection and promoting dechristianizing as agents of the
'foreign plot'. They were quickly tried and executed on 24 March
(4 Germinal). In April Chaumette followed them and the Hébertist Commune was purged. The *armée révolutionnaire* was disbanded and the Cordeliers Club ceased to wield political power.
Fear of being denounced to the Committees grew, as ordinary
workers were affected – in April an arms worker was imprisoned
for saying *'qu'il fallait que les ouvriers vivent comme les autres'*.
Surprisingly enough, the loss of the Hébertist leaders caused
confusion rather than anger among the *sans-culottes*. A police
agent reported' *'Le peuple ne veut plus se fier à personne'* – perhaps
they were coming to realize that the factions had merely made
use of them for political ends. Few have ever defended the
Hébertists: for all his violence, their leader died badly on the
guillotine. Yet, lost amongst the politics of the day there may

have been the glimmerings of what was to become twentieth-century social democracy in some of their ideas, though perhaps only Jacques Roux, who committed suicide in prison in January, really understood the social question.

If there had been a threat from the Left, there was unquestionably an attack being mounted on the Right. The policy of '*Indulgeance*' challenged the authority of the Committee and attracted to it all those whose interests were hurt by the Terror, who preferred private to public ends, and those whose morals were lax – Camille Desmoulins complained in the *Vieux Cordelier*, 'Let us beware of connecting politics with moral rejuvenation – a thing at present impracticable'. After January, the Committee was well aware of the threat and let the two conspiracies mature together. The Hébertists were struck down first because of their violent speeches in the Cordeliers Club on 4 March; and they were also men of small stature, whereas the 'Indulgents' were 'Establishment' deputies with oratorical power to challenge the Committee on the floor of the Convention. Furthermore, no doubt from a variety of motives, Robespierre hesitated to strike at Danton: it was Billaud-Varenne who pushed him into action.

Saint-Just's indictment of the Indulgents before the Convention on 31 March (11 Germinal) accused them of royalism, anti-Jacobinism (though they were Jacobins), and of debasing revolutionary government by corruption. The real issue was simply political – to destroy them before they destroyed the Committee. From the outset of their trial the Indulgents played to the gallery, for their strong point was their oratory. Even Camille Desmoulin bravely, if inaccurately, gave his age as 'Thirty-three, the same as that of the *sans-culotte* Jesus' – though he broke down at his execution. The trial lasted four days – a definite risk to the government, especially as Danton's thunderous voice was clearly heard outside the building. The trial's closure on suspicion of a prison plot to free the accused, was no surprise. It has caught the imagination of historians, no doubt because of Danton's very human character – so different from Robespierre's. But to concentrate upon the gross irregularities in the trial is to forget that what was at issue was a purge of those who intended to overthrow the Committee. At least the Dantonists did not die in the dark. The executioner on 5 April prevented Hérault de Séchelles, hitherto a member of the *Comité de Salut Public*, though a roué, from embracing Danton as he was about to mount the scaffold. 'Show my head to the people; it's worth the trouble' was Danton's last defiant gesture.

No public protest was made; the crowd seemed as indifferent as when the Hébertists died. Later historians have tried to rehabilitate 'the long decayed idol' Danton, but not even the Thermidorians reinstated the Indulgents, though they placed Marat's remains temporarily in the Panthéon. This is a measure of the decline in the moral standing of Danton, who eighteen months before had led the nation. The Germinal purges were a victory for the Committee; but, though the Convention was happy to see the end of the Hébertists, it never forgave the sacrifice of the Dantonists (though it refused to save them). Empty seats were too cold a reminder for deputies who had good reason to fear the consequences of their more corrupt actions. But by destroying, in effect, the *sans-culottes* as a political force, the Committee had put itself at the mercy of the Convention. So long as vigorous government was needed and its unity was maintained, the Committee was safe – but no longer.

In his powerful ugliness, Danton rivalled Mirabeau, and he was probably his superior in histrionic ability; yet he lacked Mirabeau's status and has impressed historians perhaps most by his virile humanity, and as the foil to Robespierre. It is not to be denied that he was venal, opportunist, inconsistent and lacking both in prolonged concentration of effort and determination of purpose. Though he saved his country in the perils of the first invasion, he was discarded in the still greater perils of the second – displaced not by a single brilliant rival, but by a Committee struggling to establish itself. He had a brilliant mind, though his legal training brought him only minor office. He rose through the Cordeliers Club to be *procureur* to the Commune, for he had a happy facility for appealing directly to the common man. Like many before him, he helped the court by offering advice, for which he was well paid; yet he played a part in the insurrection of 10 August – exactly what part has never been properly established, though he joined the Executive Council as a result. His part in 10 August is indicative of his career – he seems often to have tested 'the political wind before taking sides' (Lefebvre). Not for him those months that Robespierre spent in the political wilderness fighting a lonely battle over the war question; far rather the joys of domesticity at Arcis-sur-Aube. His defeat in Germinal, Year Two, seems to have taken him quite by surprise, for he seems not to have contemplated failure. His enemies called him the Mirabeau of the mob, and he shared with the derogated noble a capacity for quick decision where necessary and a sense of realism in which scruples had no obvious place. He was a natural orator and few of his speeches have come down to us, being mostly extemporary; but their impact seems to have been legendary. Bold and generous, it is not surprising that many Frenchmen have seen the embodiment of patriotism in him – despite his seeking peace talks. Mathiez has sought to destroy the credit of Danton's memory as much as he has promoted that of Robespierre, but it is difficult to condemn so attractively human a figure, whom, with a great deal of truth, Garat called 'un grand seigneur de sans-culottisme'.

[17] THERMIDOR

It seemed that the Germinal purges had made the Terror a vehicle for maintaining the revolutionary government in power. On 1 April Carnot had strengthened the hand of the *Comité de Salut Public* by replacing six ministries (though not Cambon's Treasury) with commissions subservient to it – a concentration of powers that both Mirabeau and Danton had desired. Most of the *répresentants en mission* were recalled, especially the worst terrorists, like Carrier, Barras, Fréron, Tallien and Fouché. But there could not yet be a relaxation of Terror until the military situation improved.

It is difficult to keep a sense of proportion about the guillotine yet most popular presuppositions about it are false. The aristo-

cracy was by no means decimated, nor did the majority of executions take place in Paris. Donald Greer (*The Incidence of the
Terror during the French Revolution*, Harvard University Press,
1951) proves that the vast majority of executions occured in the
provinces, and that there were considerable variations – 6
Départements had no executions and 45 had less than 15 each:
the great mass – 71 per cent – were in areas of civil war, where
many also died without trial (as at Nantes, Lyons or Toulon) or
fell in combat. Only 15 per cent of death sentences were passed
in Paris. There was, perhaps, a total of 35–40,000 victims, and
perhaps as many as 300,000 'suspects' (some held on ridiculous
charges) whose property was endangered. It is no wonder that
contemporaries were horrified – but the number should be compared with the 20,000 Paris *Communards* massacred in less than
a month in 1871, or the 40,000 odd shot in France in 1944. Yet
it is the Terror that everyone remembers.

One must recall the emotion of the time; the fear of invasion,
of plots, the use of the guillotine in defence of the Republic as the
'national hatchet' and the 'scythe of equality'. But of the known
deaths, only 8·5 per cent were aristocrats and 6·5 per cent clergy:
the rest were from the Third Estate. (J. M. Thompson's *French
Revolution*, pages 494–5, gives some interesting figures for the
summer of 1794.) The Terror threatened everyone, the conspira-
tor and the speculator as well as the ordinary citizen who was
resigned to obedience and without thought of conspiracy. It
went beyond 'national defence', introducing dechristianizing
and some element of the class war; but it also had a moral purpose.

The religious schism had made catholicism suspect; but there
had grown up with the Revolution a patriotic cult that had
civic virtue at its base. Robespierre desired to build upon this
civisme a religion that would check dechristianizing, restore the
'social cement' of a church, and perhaps heal the schism. In his
famous *Rapport* of 5 February 1794, he stressed the Terror's
moral rôle: 'If the basis of popular government in time of peace
is virtue, its basis in time of revolution is both virtue and terror –
la vertu, sans laquelle la terreur est funeste; la terreur, sans laquelle

la vertu est impuissante'. He was not alone on the Committee in his desire – Barère seemed to agree, and so did Billaud-Varenne, whose idea of the Terror was not much different from Robespierre's. He had most support from Couthon and Saint-Just who declared on 26 Germinal that 'revolutionary government [signified] the transition from evil to good, from corruption to probity'. It was to promote virtuous republican principles (national festivals were 'most powerful means of rejuvenation'), that Robespierre urged the establishment of a sort of State church in the *Culte de l'Être Suprême*. The Convention voted it on 7 May, and sealed the fate of dechristianizers by declaring as dogma the immortality of the soul. The *culte* was generally, if superficially, welcomed, though some secretly mocked at it and others saw it as a possible move to catholicism, as its first great festival, celebrated throughout France, was held on Whit Sunday (20 Prairial). But the overt imposition of 'morality' by the State was not to everyone's taste: it did not survive Robespierre – indeed one of the shrewdest comments on the deeper significance of 9 Thermidor was a Paris police report of 7 August: 'Prostitutes are reappearing with their customary audacity'.

The policy of strengthening central control led the *Comité de Salut Public* to present on 26 Germinal a *Rapport sur la Police Générale*, which the Convention enforced. It called to Paris all those charged with conspiracy (which may account for some of the increase in executions), although there were exceptions, like the savage *commission populaire* at Orange. It expelled from Paris and garrison towns all foreigners and nobles; but it also confused the jurisdiction over police matters exercised by the *Comité de Sûreté Générale* and the *Comité de Salut Public*, and the latter promptly set up a *Bureau de Police Générale* to supervise government servants, which Robespierre controlled at the outset. This hastened the rift between the two committees and formed part of the charge of dictatorship levelled against Robespierre.

The Terror had not removed the threat of assassination, and on 3 Prairial Admiral, perhaps intending Robespierre, nearly killed Collot d'Herbois: next day Cécile Renault was arrested when attempting to kill Robespierre. The emotion these attempts aroused recalled that on the death of Marat, and the Convention, supposing them linked with the foreign plot, on 7 Prairial declared that British troops should be allowed no quarter. The previous day Saint-Just had been summoned back from his mission with the *armée du Nord* by an urgent note, 'Liberty is exposed to new dangers ... the Committee needs to unite the knowledge and energy of all its members'. There is no direct connexion between the *Fête de l'Être Suprême* (20 Prairial) and the infamous *Loi du 22 Prairial*. It had been in preparation since 27 Germinal and was drawn up by Couthon, the man whom the Convention had earlier recalled from Lyons for his leniency. It destroyed the surviving judicial guarantees for the defence, leaving a choice between acquittal and death. Though it distinguished between ordinary crimes and conspiracy, its unnecessary violence was an irrational yielding to assassination threats: 'It is not a matter of setting a few examples', declared Couthon, 'but of exterminating the implacable henchmen of tyranny'.

The Law caused much uneasiness in the Convention for it seemed to infringe the principle of inviolability of deputies, and there was difficulty in passing it – evidence of independence that was a warning to Robespierre, and yet the Law, accelerating the Terror, was taken as further evidence of his dictatorship. It inaugurated the Great Terror of June to July, when the victims were often condemned in batches, sometimes composed of prisoners who were complete strangers to each other – though this is partly explained by the recurrent fear of a prison mutiny, for there were over 8,000 in the prisons. In the Great Terror 1,376 persons were executed in Paris as compared with only 1,251 between March 1793 and June 1794. This shook public morale, expecially as many of the victims were from the poor; the guillotine was moved to the Trône-Renversé gate and shopkeepers put up their shutters as the tumbrils passed by.

Yet this intensification of the Terror came at a time when victory seemed assured and the need for revolutionary government consequently diminished. No help had been sent to Kosciusko in Poland and the food situation at home was so strained that Car-

not commented in Germinal that they must finish it this year or
'we shall perish of hunger and exhaustion'. He urged the armies
to advance and live off enemy territory, for the committee could
not feed them for much longer. However, on 13 Prairial a grain
convoy got through to Brest after a severe engagement in which
the Brest fleet distinguished itself, and which the British, though
the convoy got through, claim as the victory of the Glorious
First of June. On 18 May Pichegru had already won an encouraging battle at Tourcoing and on 26 June, Jourdan won the major
victory of Fleurus. The Republic was no longer in danger of invasion: the two generals met in Brussels on 9 July and on the
27th (9 Thermidor) they occupied Antwerp and Liège. But victory had not brought an end to all problems, for conditions at
home were bad.

In the last months of the Terror, the government began an
active social programme – educational reforms in December
anticipating compulsory secular education; slavery abolished
in February; the February maximum to 'moralize commerce'
and help the 'virtuous trader'; the Laws of Ventôse and Barère's
Livre de la beinfaisance nationale of May forshadowing social
security (see page 156); relief for the infirm, and the disabled
beggars of Paris on 5 Prairial. It is easy to see why Babeuf thought
Robespierre had a socialist programme – indeed, some contemporaries held that it was his social programme that prompted
his overthrow by those who feared (unjustly) an attack on property. It is a strange irony that at least one factor in his fall was
that he had lost the support of the sans-culottes over the wages
policy.

The poor needed more than spiritual food: poor crops and the
disturbed situation had produced a general shortage by the
spring. The Convention might try to encourage better agricultural methods, but crops had to be requisitioned and peasants
restrained from abandoning cereals for stock-raising or crops not
subject to controls. Year Three would be a famine year: Year
Two was bad enough. Furthermore, laxity over controls brought
a return of inflation – assignats were down to 36 per cent in
Thermidor and this meant a decline in the real value of wages.

The Hébertist Commune had ignored the *maximum des salaires*; the attempt to impose it to hold prices steady, when the *maximum des denrées* was being widely evaded, undoubtedly worked to the extreme disadvantage of the worker. They struck. In April Payan imprisoned some tobacco workers for striking and in May Barère reinforced the Loi le Chapelier by threatening essential workers with the Revolutionary Tribunal if they struck. Labour was requisitioned for strike-breaking. But the wages movement gathered momentum in June and July. On 5 Thermidor the Robespierrist Commune published a fairly severe *maximum des salaires*. For this reason Guérin has called Robespierre the precursor of the Thermidorian reaction. On 9 Thermidor the masons of Hébert's old Section, *l'Unité*, talked of striking, and the Mayor of Paris, ignorant of the impending disaster, ordered the military to take special measures to control the people on the next day, a holiday. In the crisis of Thermidor there was lacking the emotion which typified earlier *journées*, and which was to reappear in Germinal and Prairial, Year Three (see pages 182-3). The *sans-culottes* failed to respond *en masse*, and those who did were ill-directed. For this reason the Convention triumphed. '*Voilà le maximum dans le panier!*' cried a worker, as Robespierre's head fell, and the next day, the members of the Commune were greeted with cries of '*foutu maximum*' as they were driven to the guillotine.

Most *sans-culottes* were ignorant of politics: the *maximum* meant stable prices to them, not a means of checking inflation or guaranteeing essential supplies for the war. When the controlled economy ceased to hold prices they withdrew support: after Thermidor the whole policy of controls collapsed. 'From this point of view, the 9 Thermidor was, indeed, a *journée des dupes* for the *sans-culottes*. . . . Ten months later, their resistance weakened by the effects of famine and the high cost of living, realizing at last what they had lost, they demanded a return to a controlled economy, rose in insurrection for the last time, only to be completely crushed and swept from the stage of history' (Soboul).

Many factors contributed to the collapse of the popular movement – five years of revolution had drained much nervous and

physical energy; conscription, as well as volunteers, drained the
young and virile, so that the movement grew old and its vigour
declined; then, too, there was a relaxation of tension after victory
at the front; the guillotine was executing ordinary folk; and the
leading *sans-culottes* had gained junior administrative office, and,
having no private income, had to be paid – they kept their job,
and income, by obeying instructions – and thus the new bureaucracy itself tended to muzzle the popular movement.

The Thermidorian coup was made possible by the collapse of
unity in the Revolutionary Government. This appeared on the
surface first in the rivalry between the two committees. Amar's
report on Chabot (see page 154) had been criticized as inadequate
by both Robespierre and Billaud-Varenne, and thereafter the
Comité de Salut Public began to take over the more important
reports, even for police matters. As early as 16 March the American ambassador had informed Jefferson that the two committees
would probably come to blows. It was Saint-Just who presented
the Reports at the Germinal trials and for the Law of 27 Germinal
– the *Bureau de Police Générale* was a standing insult to the
Comité de Sûreté Générale, which was not even consulted over the
Loi du 22 Prairial. Vadier had his revenge for this over the
Théot Affair – Catherine Théot was a harmless crackpot who
was said to have claimed Robespierre as a sort of Messiah. In
June Vadier tried to turn the case into an attack on Robespierre
and the *Culte de l'Être Suprême*: it was only with the greatest
difficulty that Robespierre got the *Comité de Salut Public* to stop
the case – a striking illustration of his lack of personal power in
the committee.

The argument had been so fierce that it was decided to move
the committee to an upper room, lest their disagreements be
overheard. For the suppressed personal conflicts within the main
committee were coming to the surface, especially as the foreign
threat diminished. Robespierre had only two close supporters,
Couthon and Saint-Just; together they were rather meaninglessly
called the 'triumvirate'. Of the rest, Prieur de la Marne and
Jeanbon Saint-André were away *en mission*; Barère was prepared
for compromise; Collot d'Herbois feared Robespierre would

attack him for his severity at Lyons; Billaud-Varenne resented Robespierre's popularity; Lindet, Prieur de la Côte d'Or and Carnot were moderate conservatives who had rallied to the *Montagnards* to save the Republic, but who hated controls and also the Ventôse laws – only Carnot was prepared to provoke a crisis, and he has a place in the intrigue leading to Thermidor. As early as 12 Germinal he had said: 'Woe to a republic in which the merit of a single man, or even his virtue, should be necessary'. In June, irritated by Saint-Just's and Robespierre's criticism of the war machine, he called them 'ridiculous dictators', and the charge was repeated after Fleurus by Collot and Billaud-Varenne. News of these disputes worried the provinces.

The disunity restored a degree of initiative to the Convention. Among the deputies were not only those who feared that their connexion with profiteers would be revealed, but also the returned *répresentants*, anxious because Robespierre might attack them for their excesses. Men like Fréron, Barras, Tallien (whose mistress, Thérésa Cabarrus was imprisoned) and Fouché had sought Robespierre's friendship on their return, but he had contemptuously rejected 'this motley gang of factionists and schemers'. (This was entirely consistent with his character, but it was a major political miscalculation.) In consequence, fearful of his ascendancy, that seemed to reach a new height with the *Fête de l'Être Suprême* and the *Loi du 22 Prairial*, they began to intrigue to save themselves from proscription. Tallien claimed the credit for organizing Thermidor, but Fouché has the better claim – '*Fouché n'était pas un Danton; il manœuvrait*' (Madelin). He was soon in contact with the dissatisfied men of the *Comité de Sûreté Générale*, and with other deputies.

Robespierre, well aware of the intrigue and deeply hurt by the accusation of dictatorship, seemed to lose all vigour and become fatalistic. On 1 July he warned the Jacobin Club that he had lost all authority in the government, and from 3 to 23 July (5 Thermidor), at the very height of the Terror, he absented himself from public life, signing only five documents that were brought round to his lodgings at the Duplays. He reappeared at the joint meeting of both Committees on 5 Thermidor, at which Barère hoped to restore unity and confidence within the government. Perhaps he doubted his colleagues' good faith (he saw particular significance in Carnot's ordering some cannon from the Paris Sections to the front); at any rate, he rejected the attempt at compromise, and without consulting Couthon or Saint-Just, precipitated the crisis by his great speech of 8 Thermidor.

No doubt he hoped to gain the support of the Plain (see page 112) for the 'national cause', and certainly the immediate impact of the speech was all he could have desired. But there now existed a strong group of deputies bound together in their opposition by the motive of self-preservation. They had shown their strength in the difficulty that had been experienced in passing the Prairial Law, and the popular revulsion against the Terror helped them. Deliberately, they celebrated victories in the field with 'fraternal banquets' that even Barère objected to as a trap. Finally, Robespierre's absence had given them the opportunity to organize themselves into a body, and so to resist the impact of Robespierre's oratory. His speech was uncompromising – it was not in his character to be a 'trimmer' – proclaiming the need for civic virtue and denouncing the intriguers *contre la liberté publique* as the real 'men of blood'. He demanded a purging of both Committees and the punishment of the 'traitors' to crush factions *pour élever sur leurs ruines la puissance de la justice et de la liberté*. But he failed to name the conspirators and his continued refusal to do so led to a stormy session in which the Order to have his speech printed was annulled. Robespierre had lost his majority. Though he repeated the speech amid great enthusiasm that night at the Jacobins, he seemed to have a presentiment of disaster and spoke of taking the hemlock of martyrdom, rejecting any appeal to force.

Next day the conspirators' plans were well laid. With the connivance of Collot d'Herbois, in the Chair, Tallien prevented Saint-Just presenting a Report and, after a violent scene, in which Robespierre was refused a hearing, Robespierre, his brother, Saint-Just, Couthon and Lebas were arrested. 'The Republic is lost, the brigands are triumphing', said Robespierre. It was over by 3 p.m. and the ineptitude of the Robespierrists during the next twelve hours sealed the Thermidorians' gamble with success. The Commune declared an insurrection and some 3,000 men, with perhaps 30 cannon, assembled, but they were so badly led by Hanriot (who was drunk) and Coffinhal, that the Convention was saved and the force itself, tired of waiting, drifted home. Robespierre refused to countenance an armed insurrection (though it was his one chance of survival) – perhaps he hoped to be triumphantly released by the Revolutionary Tribunal, like Marat, fifteen months earlier. But the Convention could not risk this, and placed its defence in the hands of Barras. Released, the prisoners went to the Hôtel de Ville, but they failed to act, and by 1 a.m. the troops in the square outside had gone home. Then Barras arrived and surprised Robespierre in the act of signing an appeal to the Sections which he had at last been persuaded to issue. Lebas committed suicide and Robespierre probably attempted to do the same, but merely broke his jaw – later Meda, who was to die, a Baron of the Empire, at Moscow in 1812, claimed to have been the maladroit assassin of the 'tyrant', but the story has never been substantiated. In the evening of 10 Thermidor, Robespierre, Saint-Just, Couthon and nineteen others were guillotined in the *Place de la Révolution*. Next day seventy-one more, mostly members of the Robespierrist Commune, perished – the largest 'batch' of the Terror.

The Thermidorians blackened Robespeirre's reputation even more effectively than the Tudors did that of Richard III. But Robespierre the ogre is pure myth, and the accusation of dictatorship will not stand close examination – yet his name is too closely associated with the Terror for him to escape blame for its excesses: even so, Napoleon, who knew him, believed he was intent on reversing the Terror. Among his friends he earned a deep devotion, but he was suspicious, cold and distant with others – a serious failing in a politician. The poor and humble recognized in him a true friend, though it would be to go too far to portray him as a 'social democrat'. Steadfastly, he refused to enrich himself during the Revolution, and his perseverance, clear sincerity, moral courage, and his 'incorruptibility', gradually brought him to a position of predominance. The long gruelling hours at the

Jacobins, in the Convention and the Committee told on his health as much as it placed him at the forefront of affairs, and he no doubt owed much, personally, to the protective skein that the Duplay household wove around him.

In a sense, it is he who personifies the moral force of the Revolution and who raises the Terror above a mere government of national defence and intimidation into a dictatorship with the characteristics of Rousseau's Legislator, imposing the General Will and forcing citizens to be free. His opponents knew that a part of his virtuous *civisme* was the avoidance of transferring political power from a corrupt monarchy to a corrupt aristocracy of wealth. It was in the spirit of a crusader, '*retranché dans sa conscience comme dans une forteresse impénétrable*' (Hamel), that he pursued the unvirtuous. As Thompson puts it: 'He was a moral fanatic, who deliberately used means he would ordinarily have disliked to attain ends that he always valued above any immediate popularity or power . . . a Calvin, but without his cramping theology'. From the young judge at Arras, who resigned because he could not pronounce the death sentence, to the spokesman of the Terror, there is a clear and logical development in his views. Yet his fall was probably at base due to his uncompromising character, that had prevented his constructing a broad party of support among the deputies, and led him to reject Barère's attempts at compromise and conciliation. In his last speech there seems almost a desire for the martyr's crown: '*Défendons le peuple au risque d'en être victimes; qu'ils courent a l'échafaud par la route du crime, et nous par celle de la vertu*' . . . '*Je suis fait pour combattre le crime, non pour le gouverner*'.

Despite the great efforts of Mathiez to rehabilitate Robespierre, efforts that historians no longer seriously contest, he lives in popular memory as the instigator of the bloodshed of the Revolution. France continues, officially, to 'ignore' his memory. It is an interesting example of the force of legend. With his death, civic virtue and idealism seem to depart from the Revolution: it is, perhaps, not to be wondered at that the period between the coups of Thermidor and of Brumaire has been so neglected by historians.

Further Reading

Many of the specialist studies of the Revolution are concerned
with the Terror and the Jacobins: much recent work has attempted to put these phenomena into clearer perspective. M. J.
Sydenham's *The Girondins* (Athlone Press, 1961) dispels the
idea of their being a party in any ordinary sense. Crane Brinton's
The Jacobins (Russell & Russell, New York, 1930) remains a
useful book. P. Caron's *La Première Terreur* (Paris, 1950) deals
with the crisis of the first invasion. For the Second Terror,
R. R. Palmer's *The Twelve Who Ruled* (Princeton University
Press, 1941) is useful, as is Sir John Elliott's *The Way of the
Tumbrils* (Rheinhart, 1958), and L. Jacob's *Les Suspects pendant
la Terreur* (Paris, 1952). For the popular movement, see A.
Soboul's *The Parisian Sans-Culottes and the French Revolution*
(Translated by G. Lewis, Oxford University Press, 1964),
George Rudé's *The Crowd in the French Revolution* (Oxford
University Press, 1959), but R. Cobb's two volumes on *Les
Armées Révolutionnaires* (Paris, 1961-3) have yet to be trans-
lated – he has published a useful article in *History* for 1957, 'The
Revolutionary Mentality in France'. Biographies abound: L.
Barthou's *Danton* (A. Michel, 1932) is good; L. R. Gottschalk's
Jean Paul Marat: a Study in Radicalism (New York, Greenberg,
1927) and Dommanget's *Jacques Roux, le curé rouge* are interest-
ing; S. J. Watson's *Carnot* (Bodley Head, 1954) is adequate but
M. Reinhard, *Le grand Carnot* (Paris, 1950) is the one to read;
E. N. Curtis's *Saint-Just* and L. Gershoy's *Bertrand Barère,
Reluctant Terrorist* (Princeton University Press, 1962), are useful.
L. Madelin's *Fouché 1759-1820* (Paris, 2 vols. reissued 1930)
establishes his place in the Thermidor crisis. On Robespierre,
perhaps the best book in English is J. M. Thompson's two-
volume *Life* (Blackwell, 1953); a much shorter book is his
Robespierre and the French Revolution (English Universities
Press, 1952). Charles Tilly's *The Vendée* (Arnold, 1964) shows the
complexities of the civil war. A. Cobban's *The Social Interpretation of the French Revolution* (Cambridge University Press, 1964)

should be read, especially as it disagrees at important points with Lefebvre and Soboul. The Revolution is put into its European context in G. Rudé's *Revolutionary Europe 1783–1815* (Fontana, 1964), in which he discounts the idea of a 'Western' or 'Atlantic' Revolution which is to be found suggested in J. Godechot's *La Grande Nation* (2 vols. Paris, 1956) and in R. R. Palmer's *The Age of the Democratic Revolution*, Vol. 1 (Princeton University Press, 1959). M. J. Sydenham's *French Revolution* (Putnam, 1965) is also useful for this section.

Principal Events, June 1792 – July 1794

FRANCE
1792

19 June. Louis vetoes Paris camp
20 June. Tuileries invaded
28 June. Lafayette returns to Paris
10 July. Girondin ministry
25 July. Arrival of Brest *Fédérés*
30 July. Arrival of *Marseillais*
10 August. Fall of Monarchy
19 August. Lafayette deserts
August–September. Emergency measures of 'First Terror'.
2–7 September. September Massacres

21 September. New Convention proclaims the Republic
October–December. Emergency measures allowed to lapse

EUROPE AND THE WAR
1792

29 April. Dillon murdered by his troops
18 May. French generals meet at Valenciennes to urge peace
100,000 Russians invade Poland
Prussia mobilizes for French war

July. Brunswick at Coblenz
28 July. Brunswick Manifesto

19 August. Brunswick crosses frontier
23 August. Longwy falls

2 September. Verdun surrenders
8 September. Brunswick enters Argonne Forest
20 September. Battle of Valmy
1 October. Prussians retreat
6 November. Battle of Jemappes

FRANCE

November–December.
  Debate on King's trial

1793
January. *Comité de Sûreté
  Générale*
21 January. Execution of
  king

February–March. *Taxation
  populaire* in Paris
8–10 March. The March Days
  in Paris
  Levy of 300,000 men
  Beginning of La Vendée
  revolt
10 March. Revolutionary
  Tribunal
18 March. Death for
  advocates of *loi agraire*

6 April. First (Dantonist)
  Comité de Salut Public
13 April. Impeachment of
  Marat
May–October. Federalist
  Revolt
4 May. First Maximum
15 May. Arrival of *Bordelais*
31 May–2 June. Jacobin
  coup overthrows Girondins

EUROPE AND THE WAR

16 November. Scheldt
  opened to navigation
19 November. Decree of
  Fraternité et secours
15 December. '*Guerre aux
  Châteaux*' decree

1793

21 January. Execution of
  king
23 January. Second Partition
  of Poland begun (takes
  until September)
1 February. War declared
  against England and
  Holland
7 March. War against Spain
  declared

18 March. Battle of
  Neerwinden
4 April. Desertion of
  Dumouriez

April–September. Second
  invasion threat
  Custine retreats from Rhine

FRANCE

3 June. Sale of *émigré* land
in small lots
24 June. Constitution of 1793
10-27 July. Second *Comité
de Salut Public* formed
13 July. Assassination of
Marat
23 August. *Levée en masse*

5 September. Attempted
Hébertist coup
9 September. *Armée
Révolutionnaire*
17 September. Law of
Suspects
29 September. Law of General
Maximum
10 October. 'Government is
revolutionary until the
peace'
October. Revolutionary
Calendar adopted
Executions of queen,
Girondins and other
political prisoners
10 November. Fête of
Reason in Nôtre-Dame
Beginning of Indulgents'
campaign against the
Terror
4 December Law of 14
Frimaire
6 December. *Liberté des
Cultes* declared
23 December. Marceau
defeats Vendéans at
Savenay

EUROPE AND THE WAR

July. Fall of Condé and
Valenciennes.
Fall of Mainz to Prussians
August. Toulon surrenders
to Hood
August–October. Kellermann
invests Lyons
September. Spaniards
besiege Perpignan
8 September. Battle of
Hondschoote

October. After retaking
Lyons, Kellermann
relieves Savoy
16 October. Battle of
Wattignies

December. Frontier fortresses
retaken.
Hoche reaches Spire
Toulon captured

FRANCE

1794

22 February. New Maximum produced

13 March. Laws of Ventôse announced

24 March (4 Germinal). Execution of Hébertists

1 April. Ministries replaced by Commissions

5 April (16 Germinal). Execution of Dantonists

16 April. *Bureau de Police Générale*

7 May. *Culte de L'Etre Suprême*

8 June (20 Prairial). *Fête de l'Etre Suprême*

10 June. Law of 22 Prairial

23 July. *Maximum des salaires*

26 July. Robespierre's last speech in the Convention

27–8 July (9–10 Thermidor) Proscription and execution of Robespierrists

29 July. Execution of Robespierrist members of Paris Commune

EUROPE AND THE WAR

1794

March. Kosciusko leads Polish rising

1 June. Battle of First of June

26 June. Battle of Fleurus End of foreign threat

26 July. Prussians begin the siege of Warsaw

27 July. Liège and Antwerp captured by Jourdan and Pichegru

PART VI
From Thermidor to Brumaire: 1794-9

[18] THE THERMIDORIAN TRIUMPH

Many historians end the Revolution at Thermidor. This is understandable, for no clear pattern emerges from the five years up to Brumaire, beyond a rejection of the Terror by politicians eagerly intriguing for power. Furthermore, the evident success of the Consulate (1799–1804) seems by contrast to augment the confusion of these years. But, while we lack the detailed historical research upon which sound judgments can be based, it is clear that much constructive work was attempted especially under the Directory: it was not solely a period of battles abroad and coups at home. The dawn of the Napoleonic era was hidden from the men of 1794: for them the Revolution had to continue, at least until the war was won.

The Thermidorians gained much from the concentrated effort of the Terror, and the victories of the early summer were extended. But the nature of the war was changing. Not only was the war effort declining, but simple aggression and conquest were replacing national defence. Different interests required a continuance of the war. While contractors grew rich, conquests provided a source of bullion and foreign currency for commercial life at home and trade abroad. The army too, had to be employed: Jacobinism was too strong within it to permit it to return in force to France, and to disband it would greatly increase the problems of food supply and unemployment (even though only

half of the paper strength of a million men were still with the
colours in 1795).

In Spain a resounding victory was gained at the Battle of the
Black Mountain in November; in the Alps a full scale invasion of
Piedmont was only prevented by the declining vigour of the
government. But, in pursuit of the policy of natural frontiers,
Jourdan was at Cologne in October. The Rhine delta held up an
advance to the north, but the incredible harshness of the 1795
winter allowed Pichegru to cross the frozen rivers and on 23
January 1795 the cavalry captured the Dutch fleet ice-bound on
the Texel. Amsterdam was occupied and the British retired to
Hanover. Belgium was reabsorbed into France and drained of
wealth, like all the conquered countries. In October it was formally annexed, but there was much controversy over annexing the
Rhineland. By the spring the impetus of the advance was stayed;
Carnot left the Committee of Public Safety in March 1795; and
there was so much desertion from the armies that France even
lost superiority in men. Furthermore, royalist propaganda was
infecting some generals – Pichegru especially.

Continued disunity among her enemies helped France. On 26
July 1794 Frederick William had laid siege to Kosciusko in
Warsaw – though it took Suvarov and the Russians to capture
the city in November. Pitt, blaming the Prussians for recent
defeats, withdrew his subsidies on 17 October, an act that did
much to ensure the collapse of the Coalition. On 25 October
Frederick William ordered negotiations to be opened with
France: these dragged on at Basel for six months and proved a
useful foil to Austro-Russian intrigue over Poland. Austria,
anxious to retain her position in the East kept an army in reserve
and eventually signed a treaty to partition Poland with Catherine
the Great on 3 January 1795. Prussia accepted the Third Partition of Poland with very bad grace on 24 October 1795.

The Treaty of Basel (April 1795), which Barthélemy negotiated for France, secured Prussian neutrality in effect for ten
years. It was a triumph, for not only had a major power recognized the Republic, but Prussia withdrew support from the
Stadtholder of Holland, thus reversing the French diplomatic

defeat of 1788 (see page 80). The Dutch in consequence concluded the Treaty of The Hague in May, ceding to France the
territory south of the Rhine, accepting a French alliance and an
army of occupation, and paying an indemnity of 100 million
florins. In October the Batavian Republic was established.
Spain made peace in July. Britain retaliated by seizing Dutch
and Spanish colonies, but though the Republic seemed victorious, the Treaty of Basel had invigorated what remained of the
Coalition. Pitt promised to Austria the subsidies that should
have gone to Prussia and, in September, Russia joined the
Coalition. A general pacification could follow now only on the
defeat or the victory of France. Though it inherited the Rhine
frontier, the Directory faced no easy foreign situation – and this
was accentuated by the treason of Pichegru, who, being in royalist pay, made an armistice with the Austrians on 31 December
1795.

At home the Thermidorians reversed the Jacobin Terror,
although some of the legislation of Year Two survived for many
months. Immediate changes were confined to the Convention
recovering control of the Executive. On 10 Thermidor the Law
of 22 Prairial was repealed and next day the *Comité de Salut
Public* suffered a major blow when, with its rival, it lost permanency by the Order requiring three of its members to be re-elected
each month none of whom was eligible to serve for the next
month. Soon only Carnot was left out of the original committee,
and he went in the spring. It lost many of its powers in August,
and the result was a speedy unwinding of the springs of government. The *sans-culottes* lost their political organization – the
Paris Commune was abolished on 27 July and the city redivided
into 12 *arrondisements* in which the bourgeoisie dominated; on
22 August the Law of 40 Sous was repealed and section meetings
reduced in number – in the following spring they had to meet on
work days. The Revolutionary Tribunal was reorganized and
eventually abolished in May 1795.

The new atmosphere in Paris was best exemplified by the appearance of frivolity among the wealthy, with many extravagances of
speech, dress and manner. *Salons* reappeared and Thérésa

Cabarrus was in her element. Former terrorists, like Fréron, Tallien and Barras, actively joined the social swing, anxious to change their spots, and they were joined by released 'suspects', reactionaries, and the families of Terror victims, anxious for vengeance. But Jacobinism was not dead: the restored freedom of the press and theatre certainly gave scope to reactionaries, and soon plays mocking the saviours of the Republic were popular – but a group of 'Neo-Hébertists' was also active, forming an Electoral Club to demand the Constitution of 1793, and led by the *enragé* Varlet and 'Gracchus' Babeuf, now editing *Le Tribun du Peuple*. Their major triumph, with the help of the surviving Jacobin sections, was to have Marat's remains placed in the Panthéon on 20 September 1794.

This was too much for the reactionaries, who had already, under the leadership of Fréron, formed the *Jeunesse dorée* (or *muscadins*), composed of lawyers' clerks, other bourgeois youth, deserters and conscription dodgers (*insoumis*). They proved very good at witch-hunting former terrorists, beating up opponents and removing the Sections from *sans-culottes* control – an early version of the German Freikorps of 1919, or of the fascist storm-troopers. Their song '*Reveil du Peuple*' temporarily rivalled the *Marseillais*. Organized violence and an attack led by Fréron resulted in the closure of the Jacobin Club in November; in the New Year the busts of Marat were broken and his body was removed from the Panthéon on 8 February 1795.

As more 'suspects' were released, and surviving Girondins and some *émigrés* returned, it became difficult to restrain the pressure for revenge. In December, Carrier was executed for his *noyades* and a commission began to investigate the terrorist activities of Barère, Billaud-Varenne and Collot d'Herbois. The government was strong enough to prevent anarchy in Paris, but it was different in the provinces. In February 1795 a massacre of Jacobins at Lyons launched the 'White Terror' directed by bourgeois, returning *émigrés* and refractory priests against Jacobins, protestants and purchasers of national lands. It was wide-spread in the South, and though it lacked the excuse, perhaps, of the September Massacres, it seems to have had deep roots – for it

was to re-appear in 1815. Its incidence varied, as had that of the
Terror; but the lynch gangs, the Companies of Jesus and the
Compagnie du Soleil, left memories as bitter as those of 1793–4.
Royalist influence was everywhere growing. The temporary pacification of the Vendée, which Hoche achieved on 17 February
1795, was so favourable to the *Chouans* that their influence was,
if anything, extended.

The slow retreat from the political aspects of the Terror was
matched by that from economic controls – indeed, it is surprising
that a free economy was not reintroduced overnight by the
Thermidorian 'hard-faced men who had done well out of the war'.
The fatal *maximum des salaires* of July 1794 was withdrawn at
the end of the month in favour of a new one, with higher wage
rates – but real wages continued to decline and in April 1795 they
were probably lower than the catastrophic level of 1789. The
Maximum was not abolished until 24 December 1794, and bread
and meat rationing, with, in some cases, requisitioning, remained.
But the abandonment of close economic controls meant severe
inflation – from which speculators and contractors benefitted,
but from which the poor, *rentiers*, small property owners and
those living on fixed incomes, suffered. It was calculated that
retail prices had risen 400 per cent by January and 800 per cent
by April 1795 over those of June 1790. The *assignats*, down to
36 per cent in July 1794, were a mere 7½ per cent in May 1795.
The dreadful winter – the Seine froze – and the disruption of
communications with the thaw, worsened conditions; naturally,
the death-rate was abnormally high and there were many sui-
cides. But there was to be no return to a Robespierrist social
democracy: instead the government failed to honour the bread
and meat ration in Paris and prices on the open market rose
incredibly – bread from 25 sous in March to 16 livres in May.
Conditions were worse in provincial towns and disorder was
common. The social question revived and provoked the final
attempt of the Parisian *sans-culottes* to gain recognition of their
needs – it was the last attempt, too, of the *Montagnards* to regain
their position in the Sections and Convention.

Agitation and strikes in government armament factories led to their closure on 8 February 1795; but the strikes gave way to food riots, aggravated by the excesses of the *muscadins* and the provocation of the wealthy, eating well while the poor starved. A dangerous class conflict, reminiscent of the massacre of the Champ de Mars, was reappearing, and the Convention arrested many agitators, including Babeuf.

The shortage of rationed bread reached famine conditions in March and there was talk of the 'sacred duty of insurrection against oppression'. On 1 April (12 Germinal) the faubourgs Saint-Marcel and Saint-Jacques marched on the Convention demanding *'du pain et la Constitution de 1793'*. They got no aid from the *Montagnards* deputies when they invaded the Assembly and the President, Boissy d'Anglas, refused to suspend the sitting. National Guardsmen from the wealthy western sections and *muscadins* easily dispersed the crowd; Paris was put under martial law under General Pichegru and there were a number of arrests, while Billaud-Varenne, Collot d'Herbois and Barère (who had done so much to organize Thermidor) were sentenced to deportation.

Conditions remained bad and royalist propaganda took full advantage – *'Prenons patience, nous aurons un roi avant quinze jours: alors nous ne manquerons pas de pain'*. But the *sansculottes* were not misled. On 20 May (1 Prairial) a much more serious rising began. It was touched off by food riots in the faubourg Sainte-Antoine and women took a principal part, as in October 1789. Once more their slogan was 'Bread and the Constitution of 1793'. An armed march on the Convention developed and this time the *Montagnards* did give some leadership when, after a deputy had been killed, the Assembly was invaded. But the intruders were ejected by volunteers from the western sections. Concessions promised next day averted what might have developed into a dangerous armed conflict. The *sansculottes* were not organized as they had been in June 1793, and on 23 May the Convention was able to surround the faubourg Sainte-Antoine. General Menou prepared to advance against the faubourg. There was much sympathy for the besieged from other faubourgs, but no practical help, and Sainte-Antoine surren-

dered without a fight. Many old scores were settled in the repression that followed. The potential leaders of future risings
were arrested, as were a number of prominent deputies – including Lindet and Jeanbon Saint-André, but when Carnot's name
was called, a deputy cried out *'mais il a organisé la victoire!'* and
he was saved. Six Jacobin deputies who had supported the insurgents were condemned: dramatically, three stabbed themselves to death and the other three, also bleeding, were guillotined, one being dead when decapitated. But there were not many
executions, though some 10,000 people were proscribed – and it
must be remembered that the loss of the breadwinner meant
starvation for his family, and often unemployment when he was
released, for it was not easy for former terrorists to find work.
The National Guard was reorganized to exclude *sans-culottes*,
placed under command of the Army, and its cannon withdrawn.

The Convention represented these *journées* as Jacobin plots,
but in fact their cause was economic hardship. Their defeat was
due to lack of political leadership and direction and to the
strength of the government: the *sans-culottes* had lost their
alliance with the radical wing of the bourgeoisie, and popular
insurrection ends with Prairial. Prairial was as big a turning
point in the Revolution as Thermidor – in a sense, it was, for the
sans-culottes, the end of the Revolution – the next popular
rising in Paris was in 1848 and sprang from origins more complex
and more 'modern' than the revolutionary *journées*.

The Convention did nothing to relieve the economic situation.
Bread supply was often below the ration allowance and frequently sold above its controlled price – for there were now no *comités
de surveillance* to prevent it. Prices on the open market reached
ludicrous proportions – sugar, 11 livres a pound in January, was
62 livres in September; firewood, 160 livres in May, cost 500
livres in September. Strikers demanding bread pertinently
asked *'Est-ce avec douze francs que nous gagnons par jour que nous
pouvons acheter du pain a quinze livres?'* The *assignat* dropped to
5 per cent in October before withering away altogether. Speculators and stock-jobbers, thriving on the inflation, did not trouble
to conceal the gap between rich and poor – Napoleon wrote to his

brother Joseph in July, 'luxury, enjoyment and the arts are resuming their sway in surprising fashion'. But the Convention was not without its attempts at reform – useful work was done in preparing for a civil code and the metric system and, despite the return to fee-paying optional education in October, secondary education was much improved, especially for medicine and engineering. However, the decision to sell *biens nationaux* without auction, if paid for within three months, had to be rescinded: the wealthy did think of the future. Many of the poor, on the other hand, turned to despair in their fight for mere survival. There was plenty of anti-republican propaganda, and some still advocated a return to Jacobin policies – '*on était plus heureux sous le règne de Robespierre; on ne sentait pas alors le besoin*'. There was talk of another *sans-culotte* rising: the strange thing was that the next *journée* found them supporting the Convention, for the crowd of the Vendémiaire crisis was composed of wealthy citizens.

Royalists, strengthened perhaps by the return of Girondin deputies, were very active. In the South they were behind the 'White Terror'; in Paris they made much of the bad conditions; abroad they continued to urge foreign invasion. Boissy d'Anglas, scarcely a royalist, was probably angling for a revival of the 1791 Constitution with the young 'Louis XVII', eldest surviving son of Louis XVI, as king. But the child died in prison on 8 June 1795, and the next legitimist heir, the Comte de Provence, now 'Louis XVIII', issued from Verona on 24 June a violent proclamation promising revenge on the revolutionaries and a return to the Ancien Régime. Twenty years later, an older and much wiser prince, with the support of foreign bayonets, he ascended the throne which he now vainly claimed by divine right.

The Verona proclamation made a restoration only possible at the hands of a foreign invasion, supported by an internal rebellion. A royalist agency in Paris had already laid plans. Pichegru, contemplating the rôle of General Monk, was in their pay. They hoped that Condé would advance from the East while the South rose in rebellion and the *Chouans*, helped by Artois and *émigrés*, would fight in the West. The plan miscarried; Pichegru did not fully cooperate, Lyons was once more put under military

rule and the prison massacres stopped and, although the British
fleet landed a force of *émigrés* on the Quiberon peninsula, Hoche
routed them on 21 July. He executed about 750 of them – 428
of them nobles. No juncture with the *Chouans* had been made,
but the result was reprisals and a renewal of the war in La
Vendée. Alarmed by this activity, the Convention arrested
royalist journalists and began to track down the *insoumis* in the
jeunesse dorée.

It was in these conditions that Boissy d'Anglas brought forward the Constitution of Year Three for a property-owning
oligarchy – 'We should be governed by the best' he said, ' . . . the
most educated and the most interested in maintaining the laws
. . . . A country governed by land-owners is in the social order;
that which is governed by non-landowners is in the state of nature'.

The new Declaration of Rights omitted the famous article,
'Men are born and remain free and equal in rights', but confirmed
economic liberty explicity and a Declaration of Duties was
added. The Constitution established a bicameral legislature, a
Council of Five Hundred (with a minimum age of thirty for
membership) to propose laws and a Council of Ancients (minimum age forty but members had to be either married or widowers)
to pass or veto them. Secondary voting excluded the dangers of
democracy, for the 30,000 electors who chose the Chambers were
to be men with property worth 200 days' labour. A third of the
Chambers was to retire annually. There was to be an Executive
of 5 Directors (aged at least forty), chosen by the Chambers,
having regulatory power, but no control over the Chambers, no
financial independence or power over the army and without the
power of veto. To this Constitution, designed to perpetuate a
conservative bourgeois republic, was added the famous Law of
the Two-Thirds, providing for the return at the first elections of
two-thirds of the existing Convention as members of the new
Chambers. This move was to ensure that there would not be a
royalist majority. The government retained enough of the Revolutionary tradition to submit the Constitution to a plebiscite.

The Constitution was approved by about a million votes to
500,000, but the Law of the Two-Thirds was approved by only

200,000 to 100,000 – it was rejected by the West, much of the South and by 47 out of the 48 Paris Sections. It was this law that gave a small group of royalists the chance to organize the *journée* of 12–14 Vendémiaire (4–6 October 1795). They were able to take advantage of popular distress, distrust at the movement of troops into the capital to control the elections, and the disgust at the Convention's attempt at self-perpetuation. But their real purpose was a royalist restoration, and their support came from the wealthy western sections that had defended the Thermidorians against Robespierre and the Convention against the *sans-culottes*. The Convention might retaliate by rearming the *sans-culottes* in self-defence (but their political organization had already been broken); but its only valid recourse was to the army. The *jeunesse dorée* rallied to the Lepeletier Section, which led the insurrection and openly proclaimed royalist aims. By 4 October some 25,000 *sectionnaires* were under arms – though only 7–8,000 joined in the attack on the Tuileries, mostly from the Lepeletier Section.

Suspecting the loyalty of General Menou, the Convention arrested him and put their trust in the man who had commanded the troops in Thermidor – Barras. Since he had only about 5,000 troops and several hundred volunteers, his position was not enviable; but he was helped by three factors – the *sans-culottes* declined to join the insurgents; the insurgents themselves showed no great stomach for a fight; and among the half-dozen generals deputed to assist Barras, was the young Bonaparte, who sent the future Marshal Murat to fetch 40 cannon. (Only afterwards was Bonaparte officially recognized as second-in-command.) He converted the Tuileries into a fortress and gave the crowd his famous 'whiff of grape-shot' that dispersed them. Next day (6 October) the engagement of Saint-Roche church was won and Barras occupied the Lepeletier Section. It was the last *journée* of the Revolution.

The royalists had been beaten and the citizens of Lepeletier, '*le foyer du royalisme, de l'agiotage et de l'anarchie*', were disarmed. By 9 October, though complaints about shortages and high prices continued unabated, Paris was quiet. The authori-

ties seemed deliberately to connive at the escape of the ring-
leaders of the insurrection – few were proscribed, and only a
couple executed. These rebels were forgiven, those of Prairial
were not: it is difficult to avoid the conclusion that this was simply class distinction, for the Vendémiaire 'mob' was a stranger to
manual work. It is ironic, too, that Fréron, the original organizer
of the *jeunesse dorée*, should be sent to the South to stop the
'White Terror'.

Even so, the *sans-culottes* continued to suffer throughout the
winter; hopelessness and hunger had so destroyed their spirit that
there were even very few instances of *taxation populaire*. Furthermore, there was now a new factor in Parisian life – the army
stayed in occupation to keep order. The surviving Thermidorians
had defeated their twin enemies of social democracy and royalist
restoration, and they dissolved the Convention on 26 October,
with a general amnesty for all 'activities arising directly from
the Revolution'. If the wealthy conservative bourgeiosie retained power, already in the wings stood the candidates for the
rôle of military dictator – though as yet no one would have
thought of Bonaparte.

[19] THE DIRECTORY

Instability, plots and coups are common features of the Directory, and it was to be swept away by Napoleonic glory: but it
has suffered unjustly at the hands of historians. From the Convention it had inherited an impossible financial situation, with
rampant inflation and a worthless currency. Conquered countries had to be used as a source of finance – the Directory did not
begin this policy, and in any case the generals would have mulc-
ted their conquests themselves. At home its officials were no
more corrupt than those of other countries – though there may
have been greater opportunities in France. But during its four
years of life, it was not idle, even if it failed to find solutions to
the major problems facing it, or to prevent the military dictatorship, with which it was always threatened, from destroying it.

At first there were 413, later raised to 511 former members of the Convention in the new Chambers. There were few dominant personalities and the lack of any predominant party group prevented the adoption of firm policies. The royalists remained strong, but the main group of politicians was the Right Wing *Clichiens* (called after their Club de Clichy). The five Directors were Revellière-Lépeaux, Reubell, Barras, Letourneur and finally Carnot – it had been intended to have Sieyès, the 'mole of the revolution', who, having 'existed' during the Terror, had emerged to play an active, if not wholly constructive, part in affairs, but he declined. The Directory had no more cohesion so far as personalities were concerned than had the Great Committee of Public Safety, but it lacked both the powers and the vigour of its predecessor.

The legend that the Directory was ineffective (perhaps merely inadvertently created by the contrast with the Consulate), is particularly unjust in the economic field. A firmer policy, tempering laissez-faire with state intervention and stronger administrative control, succeeded the wild scramble of Thermidorian speculation. In Paris many were saved from starvation by the distribution of food which continued to be requisitioned for the big towns and army. The embezzlements of Barras, Talleyrand (who returned from exile in England and America in 1796) and their banker friends, were a national scandal, but the government restored a control over foreign exchange and the stock market to stop speculative excesses. On 19 February 1796 the *assignats* were discontinued, but a bold attempt to stabilize the paper currency on 18 March miscarried. *Mandats territoriaux* for the direct purchase, without auction, of national lands were issued: but severe depreciation meant much good land went for ridiculous sums and the scheme had to be stopped on 6 November. Thereafter a return to a metallic currency was attempted and this prevented inflation reaching the ludicrous heights of the German mark after the First World War. But it was still dependent on bullion from captured countries, for there was little specie circulating in France. A high tariff, for protective, revenue and military purposes, developed and was to provide the

basis of Napoleon's Continental System. Furthermore the
government promoted industry (as the Consulate was to do) by
encouraging invention, useful arts, research and improvements
in canals and roads.

Much work was done to stabilize finances; in September 1797
Ramel's budget changes cut back government spending and
'liquidated' two-thirds of the public debt. Direct taxes were
revised and an attempt made to recover unpaid taxes. In 1798 a
new system of tax assessments and collection by trained civil
servants, was adopted – indeed the Directory created in embryo
the Napoleonic bureaucracy and laid the foundations for the
stability for which the Consulate (1799–1804) has taken full
credit. But the rehabilitation of the Directory must not go too
far – since taxes came in slowly, it was forced to resort to ex-
pedients, well known under the Ancien Régime, (before 1798 its
accounts were chaotic) to pay its contractors, who calculated
their prices accordingly in terms of risks. Its officials were corrupt
and its deflationary policy, though necessary, hurt many private
citizens. Its good intentions were checked by the decline in
public service and lack of money. Yet it struggled against mani-
fold difficulties in a period of some confusion and readjustment,
and therefore should not be condemned too easily. In particular,
its work for education should be noted; it laid the foundation for
nineteenth-century public education, which Condorcet had
championed. The Polytechnic, the Lycées, the *école centrale* and
école normale all took root in these years.

From the outset the Directory was dogged by instability and
the need precariously to maintain support in the Chambers, for
it was perpetually under fire. In October 1795, in reaction to the
new constitution, the Club du Panthéon was formed to promote
social democracy. It circulated its own paper, *Tribun*, edited by
Babeuf. Carnot, moving further and furthur to the Right, was
determined to crush a potentially anarchic organization and had
Bonaparte close the Club in February 1796. Babeuf and Buonarotti (the friend of Robespierre) retaliated by forming an actual
insurrectionary committee to prepare a final revolt by the *sans-
culottes* to gain economic equality. Prices were still rising: bread, 45

livres a pound in December 1795, was 80 in May and meat had risen almost as much.

The Babouvists wanted the Constitution of 1793 and a Republic of Equals. Their views were extreme; Buonarotti regarded the Ventôse Laws (see page 156), *'le vaste plan d'une réformation'*, as the germ of the *Égaux* programme with its accent on collective ownership, especially of land, *'qui n'est à personne'*. Preparations for the rising were very thorough. A small directory knew all the plans; its agents received their instructions – and the agents were quite widely spread in the police and army. The movement received some respectable support from Amar and Lindet, Robespierre's old enemies, but they did not accept its full social programme. It was betrayed, and crushed by Carnot – not with Bonaparte's aid, for on the day the *Conspiration des Égaux* was nipped in the bud, the future Emperor was fighting the Battle of Lodi. 131 persons were arrested and 30 shot out of hand on 10 May 1796. Babeuf, exhibited in a cage, was tried in February 1797 and, after a spirited defence that lasted three months, he was guillotined on 27 May. Later, Buonarotti did much to publicize Babeuf's ideas, and they were not without influence upon Italian and Russian revolutionaries, and on the English Chartists. Indeed, Buonarotti's book on Babeuf became a 'set text' for nineteenth-century revolutionaries. But the movement itself, in the world of 1796, was insignificant – though Babeuf's followers did provoke a mutiny at Grenelle in September 1796, which was severely repressed. The Conspiracy has, perhaps, been exaggerated; it was certainly not the 'last episode of the revolution' (David Thomson), though it is an important point for those who believe in the doctrine of the 'continuing revolution'.

Royalist intrigue, often associated with British money and spies, continued and the abbé Brottier was imprisoned for a plot in January 1797. However, the Directory struggled on, though, in the words of a police agent, the people *'continue à vomir mille imprécations contre la gouvernement'*.

Surprisingly enough, despite Bonaparte's great success in Italy, there was a landslide victory for the Right at the elections of April 1797. Carnot's position was not thereby strengthened, for his ally, the Director Letourneur, was replaced by Barthélemy who proved to be ineffective as an intriguer. For the Republicans, the biggest danger was of the Right depriving the Directors of executive powers and thus preparing the way for a restoration – especially when Pichegru became President of the Five Hundred and, shortly afterwards, Bonaparte discovered proof of his treasonous correspondence with the royalists. Only the army could ensure Republicans against a restoration. In July 1797 Barras placed Talleyrand in the Ministry of Foreign Affairs and General Hoche was temporarily and illegally made Minister of War and transferred a sizeable force to Paris. It was apparent that another coup was in preparation. Bonaparte, in Italy, refused to intervene, but sent the brusque Augereau who was put in charge of the Paris garrison: '*Je suis arrivé pour tuer les royalistes*', he said. The Right was organizing the wealthy sections for another Vendémiaire, but Barras and his friends moved quickly, occupying Paris on 17–18 Fructidor (3–4 September) and arresting Barthélemy, Pichegru and others – Carnot, forewarned, escaping to Switzerland. The royalists and Right were immobilized and a purge of the Chambers followed – 17 were deported (Pichegru escaping). Opposition newspapers were suppressed, censorship restored and measures taken against returned *émigrés* and priests. The coup of 18 Fructidor had restored a sort of dictatorship; but the Chambers, though cowed, cooperated no more easily than did the Convention with the Committee of Public Safety after June 1793. The rôle of the army had been clearly demonstrated, and Bonaparte, though absent, had established a claim to be the military dictator of the future. As Madelin puts it, '*la loi devint le sabre* ... [*et*] ... *a fait Napoléon*' – if Barras had acted less speedily, there might well never have been a Napoleonic era. However, some six months later (11 May 1798) the Directory had once again to purge the Chambers after unfavourable electoral returns – but this scarcely deserves the name of the 'coup' of 22 Floréal.

Despite instability at home, the Directory pursued an aggressive policy abroad, though the Rhenish campaign of 1795 had not been a very great success. But the policy of founding sister republics (of which the Batavian Republic was the first) beyond France's natural frontiers was begun. A vigorous campaign was planned for the spring of 1796, lest the Coalition find revived strength. Carnot intended the main attack to be on Vienna across Southern Germany, under Jourdan and Moreau, with a minor campaign under Kellermann and Shérer in the Alps and Lombardy. On 2 March 1796, however, Bonaparte succeeded Shérer and this changed the whole nature of the plan. Furthermore, both Moreau and Jourdan were defeated and driven back across the Rhine by October 1796, thus releasing Austrian troops for Italy.

Bonaparte's incredible success forced the Piedmontese to sign the Armistice of Cherasco on 28 April 1796, and resulted in the conquest of Lombardy after the Battle of Lodi on 10 May. After the Battle of Rivoli (14 January 1797), the rest of the peninsula lay open to him. Piedmont was annexed and the coastal strip round Genoa made into the Ligurian Republic (June 1797). To prevent them declaring themselves independent republics, the Central Duchies were combined into the short-lived Cispadane Republic, which was absorbed into the Cisalpine Republic including Lombardy and some Papal territory, in July. Much bullion and many art treasures, systematically chosen, flowed to Paris – after the fall of the ancient Venetian Republic in May, the great horses of Lysippus from St Mark's cathedral joined the spoil. The campaign came to a timely conclusion at the Treaty of Campo Formio (a month after the Fructidor coup) on 17 October, when, with a fine disregard for protocol, Bonaparte made a general peace with Austria, who recognized the Rhine frontier for France (thus surrendering Belgium) and exchanged conquered Lombardy for Venetia – an exchange which Bonaparte had no authority to make. On his return to Paris on 10 December 1797 he was the hero of the hour.

He was put in command of the Army of England in December 1797. The war with England had dragged on without credit to the French, although peace negotiations had been going on intermittently since 1796. The Spanish declaration of war against Britain forced Admiral Jervis to evacuate the Mediterranean in

the Autumn of 1796, but he defeated the Spanish fleet off Cape
St Vincent on 14 February 1797. Duncan defeated the Dutch
fleet at Camperdown on 11 October. Meanwhile attempts to aid
Wolfe Tone in Ireland were checked when bad weather prevented Hoche sailing to Bantry Bay in December 1796, and a small
force that landed in Pembroke in February 1797 surrendered.
Eighteen months later Humbert met with no greater success
when he landed in Ireland in September 1798. By that time the
peace negotiations at Lille had been broken off, for the Right,
defeated in the Fructidor coup, was suspected of being linked
with Pitt's 'foreign plot'. Strong measures were taken against
British trade by the Law of 29 Nivôse (18 January 1798) which
authorized the seizure of any merchantman carrying anything of
British origin – a precursor of the Milan Decree of 1807. For his
part, Bonaparte exchanged the command of the Army of England for that of Egypt and set sail (evading Nelson's blockade) on
19 May 1798. '*Il est enfin parti*', breathed Barras.

The creation of sister republics continued; in April Switzerland became the Helvetic Republic, and in February (the Pope
being imprisoned) the Roman Republic was declared. After an
ill-advised attack on Rome, the Bourbons were driven out of
Naples and the Parthenopean Republic founded in January
1799. All the new republics lost money and art treasures to France
and received constitutions (there were ten in all) based on that of
Year Three.

During the later months of 1798 the Second Coalition was in
the process of being formed. French activity in Switzerland,
Italy, Egypt and the Levant had aroused great suspicion and
not a little fear. Furthermore, the Tsar Paul, who had succeeded
Catherine the Great in 17 November 1796, was offended that Bonaparte should take Malta from the Knights of St John, for the
Tsar was the patron of the Order. The war opened disastrously
for France. Jourdan was forced back across the Rhine in March
1799 and, on 27 April, Suvarov routed Moreau at Cassano and
entered Milan and Turin. On 15 August he defeated and killed
Joubert at Novi – North Italy was now in Coalition hands. Then
on 19 September the Duke of York, with an Anglo-Russian army,

landed in Holland. Once more the chance to destroy the Revolution was available to its enemies. But the old disagreements prevented united action and the chance quickly passed for, on 26 September, Masséna won at Zurich and Suvarov withdrew. On 18 October York evacuated Holland and on 22 October Paul announced his withdrawal from the Coalition. But on 9 October Bonaparte, having left his army in Egypt, landed at Fréjus in order to save France from invasion – but the 'saviour' had arrived too late: France was no longer in danger.

Internally, the Directory continued its uncertain course. There was a great deal of civil disorder, and a fresh outbreak in La Vendée was feared. On 20 May 1799 Sieyès, notoriously opposed to the Directory, with the help of Barras, replaced Reubell as a Director. Together, Sieyès and Barras effected the 'coup' of 30 Prairial – it was really no more than a change of ministry – by replacing their three colleagues with two supporters, Roger Ducos and Moulin, an obscure Jacobin general. More generals, including Bernadotte, the future Crown Prince of Sweden, became ministers and the appointment of Robert Lindet, a former member of the Committee of Public Safety, as Minister of Finance, seemed to indicate that a Jacobin government of national defence was about to be formed – for the surviving Jacobins had been angrily accusing the Directory of allowing counter-revolution to play into enemy hands and of wantonly provoking the renewed war, without any preparations having been made. There were vague echoes of 1792 in all this. Censorship was relaxed and clubs reopened – the most famous being that at the Manège where Drouet, the hero of the flight to Varennes and a collaborator of Babeuf, presided – '*Babeuf et ses complices étaient, aussi bien, salués à la tribune comme de "vertueux martyrs"* ' (Madelin).

By stressing the danger to the Republic, the Jacobins passed several emergency measures recreating something approaching revolutionary government. On 28 June 1799 Jourdan secured a form of a *levée en masse*, and a further reorganization of the National Guard began in July. Requisitioning increased and a forced loan of 100 millions was imposed, especially on rich

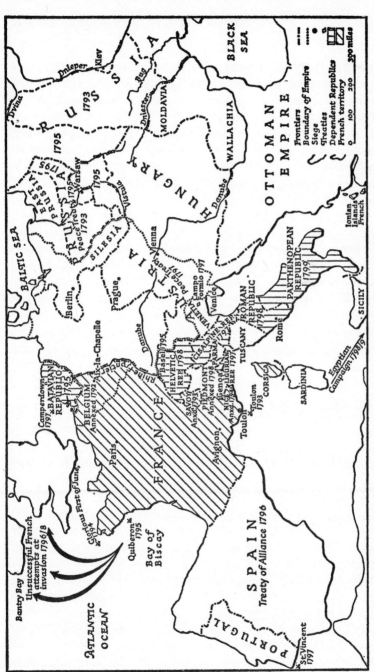

EUROPE IN 1799 (cf. map on page 79). *Note the expansion of France and the altered frontiers in Eastern Europe*

speculators. On 12 July came the *loi des ôtages* requiring hostages
from families of rebels and *émigrés* in those departments declared
to be in a state of 'disturbance'. This was too much for those who
'feared the mass of republicans more than the hoards from the
north' (as Lamarque, a Girondin, put it). The *jeunesse dorée* revived and attacked the Manège, and there were similar disturbances in other towns. Some departments were in the greatest
disorder – a royalist rising broke out in the Upper Garonne area,
and another *Chouannerie* appeared – Le Mans and Nantes were
seized in October. The Jacobins hoped to arouse popular support,
but they lacked the means of organizing it. Furthermore, the
government maintained a garrison of 20,000 in Paris, and Sieyès
had no intention of launching a Jacobin dictatorship. In July
Fouché had taken over the Ministry of Police and in August he
closed the Manège Club. Sieyès was looking for a general to
complete his coup, but Joubert, his first choice, was killed at
Novi, on 15 August. Then the sudden victories of September
changed the situation; the national danger was over in a few
weeks and there was no need now of Jacobin emergency measures.
Perhaps it was the coup of Brumaire that saved the Jacobins
from proscription.

But Brumaire was not the coup that Sieyès was planning;
rather he sought a revision of the Constitution by a military
'take-over'. It is odd that he thought he could prevent thereby
a military dictatorship. Talleyrand played his part in bringing
Bonaparte and Sieyès together, and other generals gave their
support. On 18 Brumaire (9 November 1799) the Elders voted to
move to Saint-Cloud because of a supposed terrorist plot, and to
put Bonaparte in command of the Paris garrison. Next day,
after a peculiarly ill-managed coup, the Directory was replaced
by three Consuls – Bonaparte, Sieyès and Roger Ducos. If the
dupes of Thermidor were the *sans-culottes*, Sieyès was the dupe
of Brumaire: by the end of the year he had ceased to be Consul.

The coup had been far from a resounding success in its
execution, but its results were patently clear. At last the military dictator had stepped upon the stage, in full control and yet
to some extent the prisoner of the Revolution to which he owed

his rise. The Napoleonic era has a glory and fascination all its own, but its foundation was firmly lodged on the achievements of the Revolution – yet its greatness is rightly personified in Napoleon, who provided that motive force that other leaders had lacked: '*au cours de cette période, d'ailleurs si brève, tout paraît s'effacer devant lui, c'est lui qui même l'histoire*' (Lefebvre).

Early in its course the Revolution gave a foretaste of that 'satanic power' that so frightened contemporaries; yet Burke exaggerated when he condemned the changes up to 1790 as destructive of traditional society. The really new changes, that were to release dynamic forces in the future, came almost by accident in the emergency government of the Terror, when, for a short while, appeared the prototype of a modern totalitarian state with a policy leaning far towards social democracy. The significance of this was lost on contemporaries, who viewed the Terror as a period of bloodshed inimical to duly constituted authority. It was no wonder that they came to fear the Revolution and to think of it as a holocaust rudely shattering the stability of their world in a river of blood. This literary tradition has become less and less tenable as historians, with the benefit of hindsight, have come to recognize that the Revolution, like 1914, did not so much bring changes as accelerate currents of development already flowing. The Terror, so necessary to the survival of the Republic, so 'modern' in a very real sense, was regarded by the bourgeoisie as a short-term dictatorship to be discarded as soon as practicable. In assessing the changes, apart from those of the Terror, historians have been led almost to question the uniqueness of the French Revolution, pointing to movements for reform of a similar nature to the changes of 1790 in contemporary Europe and America – Professor Cobban has even hinted that the whole Revolution may be largely the creation of politicians and historians.

But the Revolution will not be so easily dethroned. It created a new structure of society – albeit one already implicit in the long-term changes of the eighteenth century. In the first instance, the Ancien Régime was swept away and the king lost

the Divine Right to his sovereignty, for the Rights of Man
placed the sovereignty of the State within the hands of its
politically equal citizens. In this new 'secularized' state, the
Church lost its corporate privileges and, as an institution,
suffered more than is often realized. The nobility, to the joy of
the peasants, lost their seigneurial rights and became ordinary
citizens. With the far-reaching social revolution implicit in the
career open to talents, they suffered a fundamental loss of
prestige as well as of the monopoly of administrative offices. But
feudalism was in decay before 4 August dealt it a mortal blow
and, for all the sale of national lands, the pattern of land-owner-
ship did not change radically: there were fewer vast estates,
but the nobility – even the *émigrés* – were not dispossessed, and
Ferrières was not the only noble to remain in France and survive
the Terror. The aristocrats who crept back under the Empire, or
returned at the Restoration, were not destitute. As to the peasants, the wealthier ones gained more land and farmed well,
sometimes with new methods; but the majority remained too
poor, too lacking in cohesion or political consciousness to benefit
much from the Revolution beyond gaining their freedom from
the feudal reaction. However, though the deputies themselves
believed in new agricultural methods, the Assemblies did not
dare resort to enclosure: the peasant revolt of the summer of
1789 was sufficient warning to them. The Revolution was, after
all, predominantly urban, where the lack of an effective police
force or reliable troops gave an additional significance to any
sudden riot. But the urban poor gained little from the Revolution,
apart from the release of dynamic economic forces that might
have atrophied under the Ancien Régime, and the chance to
make their way in the world, given ability and good luck. The *sans-
culottes* were vital for the development of the Revolution, but
their leanings towards social democracy made them too dangerous
for the bourgeois politicians to share political power with them.

The real gainers from the Revolution were the bourgeoisie as
a whole, who had gained the right to claim any office in the State.
Their views on laissez-faire were greatly to help the development
of nineteenth-century capitalism and after the experience of

the Terror, state control of the economy was relaxed. With
access to education they could enjoy the real benefits of the
political equality that they had gained. In the new France old
barriers were swept away and a real national unity was achieved,
with a common language, administration, legal system and
weights and measures – well might Tocqueville claim that the
Convention had achieved what the Capetians had failed to do
in nine hundred years. The bourgeoisie would have preferred to
run their affairs locally, but the war committed them to dictatorship, and they preferred the military dictatorship of a Napoleon
to the incipient social democracy of the Year Two. In any case,
the greater centralization of government created many administrative posts for which they were obvious candidates. Women
were not emancipated, least of all by the Jacobins, hostile to
immorality in private life. Men were free politically, yet the
State claimed them for military service – conscription became a
permanency with Jourdan's Law of 19 Fructidor, Year Six
(5 September 1798).

If there was much continuity between the period before the
Revolution, and the Revolution itself, the France of the Consulate and Empire is nearer to that of today than was Louis XVI's.
Contemporaries were ignorant of such continuity and regarded
the Revolution as a great shock to existing society: Pitt imposed
repressive measures and, in Austria, Collerado developed the
secret police organization for which Metternich was later to
claim the credit. The Revolution will not be denied 'its full
tragic stature as the profound social convulsion from which
modern Europe was born'. Within France the struggle left deep
wounds that Napoleon was unable to heal and which were to
reopen from time to time in the future.

Further Reading

The period after Thermidor is sparsely covered. The best general
books, though they are advanced, are by Georges Lefebvre *The
Thermidorians* (Routledge, 1966), *The Directory* (Routledge,
1966), and *Napoléon* (Volume XIV of the series *Peuples et*

Civilisations, Presse Universitaire de France, 1953). M. Reinhard's *La France du Directoire* (2 vols. Paris, 1956) is thorough. For the defeat of the popular movement, see a detailed study by K. D. Tönnesson, *La Défaite des Sans-Culottes* (Paris, 1959). G. Rudé's article in *Economic History Review* (April 1954) on Prices and Wages, is useful. For Babeuf, see David Thomson's *The Babeuf Plot* (Routledge 1947). J. L. Talmon's *The Origins of Totalitarian Democracy* (Secker and Warburg, 1952) is thought-provoking. For the results of the Revolution, see J. Godechot's *Les institutions de la France sous la Révolution et l'Empire* (Paris, 1951); P. Farmer, *France Reviews its Revolutionary Origins* (Columbia University Press, 1944); and A. Cobban's *The Myth of the French Revolution* (H. K. Lewis, 1955).

Principal Events, July 1794 – November 1799

FRANCE

1794

27 July. Paris Commune suppressed

28 July. Law of 22 Prairial repealed

31 July. *Maximum des salaires* withdrawn

22 August. Law of 40 sous repealed

12 November. Jacobin Club closed

24 December. Maximum abolished

1795

February. 'White Terror' breaks out in South

17 February. Hoche temporarily pacifies La Vendée

5 March. Carnot leaves Committee of Public Safety

1 April. *Journée* of 12 Germinal

THE WAR

1794

17 October. Pitt withdraws subsidies to Prussia

25 October. Frederick William authorizes negotiations with France

9 November. Suvarov takes Warsaw

1795

8 January. Austro-Russian agreement on Third Partition of Poland

23 January. Pichegru captures Dutch fleet Amsterdam occupied

2 March. Pichegru at Mainz

5 April. Prussia makes peace at Basel

FRANCE

20–23 May. *Journée* of
Prairial
8 June. Louis 'XVII' dies in
prison
24 June. Louis 'XVIII'
issues reactionary
proclamation from Verona
27 June. *Émigrés* land at
Quiberon Bay
20 July. Hoche routs
invaders, but provokes
another *chouannerie*
Boissy d'Anglas introduces
Constitution of Year Three
22 August. Law of Two-
Thirds
4–6 October. Rising of
Vendémiaire

26 October. Convention
dissolves itself
The Directory
Club du Panthéon formed

1796
February. Carnot has
Bonaparte close Club du
Panthéon
18 March. Scheme for
Mandats territoriaux
(miscarries)

10 May. *Conspiration des
Égaux*

THE WAR

16 May. Holland makes
peace at The Hague

22 July. Spain makes peace

October. Belgium annexed;
Batavian Republic formed
24 October. Prussia accepts
Third Partition of Poland
31 December. Pichegru makes
an armistice with the
Austrians

1796

2 March. Bonaparte succeeds
Shérer as general of the
armée d'Italie
28 April. Piedmont makes
Armistice of Cherasco
10 May. Bonaparte defeats
Austrians at Lodi
June. Jourdan and Moreau
advance into South
Germany

FRANCE

September. Mutiny at
   Grenelles

THE WAR

August. Franco-Spanish
   treaty of alliance forces
   Jervis to leave
   Mediterranean
October. Jourdan and
   Moreau forced back across
   Rhine (Austrian troops
   released for service in Italy)
16 November. Bonaparte's
   victory at Arcola
December. Bad weather
   prevents Hoche's
   expedition to Bantry Bay

1797
14 January. Bonaparte's
   victory at Rivoli
January. Royalist plot by
   Abbé Brottier

1797

14 February. Jervis defeats
   Spanish fleet off St Vincent
22 February. Failure of
   invasion of Pembroke
April. Venice occupied

27 May. Babeuf executed

June. Ligurian Republic
July. Cisalpine Republic

4 September. Coup of 18 Fructidor preserves the Republic
30 September. Ramel's 'bankruptcy of the two-thirds'

11 October. Duncan defeats
   Dutch fleet at Camperdown
18 October. Bonaparte makes
   Treaty of Campo Formio
10 December. Bonaparte
   returns to Paris

1798
January. Draconian Law of 29
   Nivôse against British commerce

1798

FRANCE

11 May. 'Coup' of 22 Floréal
   excludes 48 opposition
   deputies

5 September. Jourdan's General Law of Conscription

1799

20 May. Sieyès joins the
   Directory
18 June. 'Coup' of 30 Prairial
   Jacobin measures to meet
   serious foreign threat
12 July. *Loi des Otages*

October. A new *chouannerie*
   breaks out – Le Mans and
   Nantes taken
9 October. Bonaparte lands
   at Fréjus

9 November. *Coup d'état of*
   18 Brumaire

THE WAR

February. Roman Republic
12 April. Helvetic Republic

18 May. Bonaparte sails for
   Egypt, taking Malta
   en route
1 August. Battle of the Nile

November. Naples attacks
   Roman Republic
   Second Coalition formed

1799
January. Naples occupied
   and proclaimed the
   Parthenopean Republic
March–May. Bonaparte
   vainly besieges Acre
March. Jourdan forced back
   across Rhine

15 August. Suvarov defeats
   and kills Joubert at Novi
19 September. Duke of York
   lands in Holland
26 September. Masséna
   victorious at Zurich

18 October. York withdraws
   from Holland
22 October. Tsar Paul
   withdraws from coalition

Appendix I

GLOSSARY OF FRENCH TERMS
USED IN TEXT

accapareur: one who hoards, generally foodstuffs, often a
    Parisian grocer.
Ancien Régime: traditional government and society before 1789.
Appelants: those deputies, who in January 1793 wished to
    submit the question of the king's fate to a plebiscite.
armée révolutionnaire: citizen army of Jacobins and *sans-
    culottes* raised in various cities in September 1793 primarily
    for compelling farmers to release crops for the towns.
    Discredited and disbanded on fall of the Hébertists.
assignats: revolutionary paper money issued on the backing of
    national lands.
Austrian Committee of the Tuileries; group of royalists about
    the queen suspected (rightly) of plotting the overthrow of
    the Revolution.
cahiers de doléances: lists of grievances prepared severally by
    each of the three Estates in preparation for the Estates
    General of 1789.
certificate de civisme: documentary evidence of civic virtue and
    political orthodoxy, important in towns in the Terror (q.v.).
commissionaires aux accaparement: Officers appointed by the
    Sections (q.v.) to ensure effective operation of the Maxi-
    mum and to investigate charges of hoarding food.
comités révolutionnaires: created 21 March 1793 (originally
    comités de surveillances), to assist in police and security
    work, after Thermidor they become *comités d'arrondise-
    ments.*
Commune: the revolutionary local government authority of
    Paris, formed in July 1789. Disbanded after Thermidor;
    reappears briefly in 1848 and 1870.
complot aristocratique: suspicion that nobles would overthrow
    the Revolution by fomenting civil war or inviting foreign

invasion. Appears in 1789, and becomes a fundamental
factor in the 'revolutionary mentality'.

culottes dorées: the wealthy, as opposed to less wealthy citizens
– literally, fancy breeches.

décade: the ten-day week introduced by the revolutionary
calendar, each tenth day being a *décadi*.

déroger: to lose caste, to forfeit the rank of noble.

le droit à l'existence: the *sans-culotte* ideal that everyone should
receive enough for his family to be saved from hunger.

l'égalité des jouissances: the *sans-culotte* ideal that all should
have equal opportunity to enjoy those benefits that
society confers on its members – hence the right to public
relief and free public education. (Such ideas have become
the commonplace of twentieth-century advanced societies.)

émigré: one who emigrated from France to avoid the Revolution, not necessarily a noble, but usually one.

enragé: followers of Jacques Roux and Varlet, violent denun-
ciators of speculators and hoarders, suspected of preaching
the *loi agraire* (q.v.).

Federalism: the idea that each local area should be responsible
for running its own affairs. The Girondins were advocates
of this ideal, but it detracted from the 'unity of the
Republic'.

fédérés: armed units of citizens from the provinces who came
to Paris to celebrate the National Festival of 14 July, and
who played a vital part in the Fall of the Throne (10
August 1792). They were also involved in the conflict
between Girondins and Jacobins.

Feuillants: originally moderate members of the Jacobin Club,
who broke away in July 1791, when republican ideas
became common in the Club. They hoped to save the
monarchy for a moderate constitutional monarchy of their
own devising.

insoumis: citizens who endeavoured to avoid conscription.

intendants: important local officers under the king during the
Ancien Régime, through whom the king controlled the
country.

jacquerie: a violent rising of the peasants.

jeunesse dorée: bands of anti-Jacobin youths, with a tendency to thuggery, organized by Fréron after Thermidor. One of their purposes was, in modern parlance, 'to keep the workers down'. They were defeated in the Vendémiaire crisis of 1795. Sometimes called *muscadins.*

journée: name given to an important day, generally when an action of great political consequence occurred, e.g. 14 July 1789.

lettre de cachet: a royal writ allowing the king to imprison without showing cause and without trial. At the beginning of the century it was an instrument of arbitrary power, but had ceased to be so, in effect, by the time of Louis XVI.

lit de justice: a special session of the Paris Parlement by which the king could oblige the registration of his decrees.

loi agraire: the idea of forcibly subdividing large estates (and also other property) into smaller units to produce a more equitable distribution of wealth. It was feared as inimical to property rights, and was one of the reasons for the severe treatment of working-class movements by the bourgeoisie.

Marais: see Plain.

marc d'argent: the property qualification for deputies under the 1791 Constitution.

Maximum: the declaration of a maximum price for particular goods. *Maximum des denrées,* fixed maximum price for foodstuffs, *Maximum des salaires,* fixed maximum for wages.

menu peuple: the poorer classes, generally the urban proletariat.

métayage: a system of leasing farms where the owner receives part of the crops produced by the lessee.

muscadins: see *jeunesse dorée.*

non-jurors: priests who refused to take the Oath of Fidelity to the Civil Constitution of the Clergy in 1790. They were generally associated with counter-revolution, but not necessarily so.

pacte de famine: practice, popularly attributed to royal governments and merchants, of withholding supplies of corn until
prices reached famine level.

Parlements: the ancient law courts of which the Paris Parlement was by far the most important. They had acquired
considerable political power and played a part in the
révolte nobiliaire.

Père Duchesne: popular newspaper, edited by Hébert, distributed free among the troops at the fronts. It was demagogic
and extremist.

philosophes: the name given to the writers and thinkers of the
mid-eighteenth century.

physiocrats: the name given to a group of *philosophes* concerned
with problems of economics. Their leader was Quesnay,
and they claimed Turgot as a disciple.

Plain: the large group of deputies in the Convention who were
not committed to either Girondins or Jacobins, but on
whom the Jacobins came to depend for their majority.
Robespierre fell because he temporarily lost their support.
They are also known as the *Marais.*

portion congrue: the stipend which parish priests received.

représentants en mission: deputies chosen by the Convention,
sometimes the Committee of Public Safety, to fulfil
certain liaison and other duties in the provinces or with
the armed forces.

Réunion des Ordres: the joining together in a single Assembly
of the Three Estates of the Estates General. It occurred
in June 1789, and its consequence was the triumph of
the Third Estate.

révolte nobiliaire: the active resistance of nobles and *Parlements*
to royal attempts at reform in 1787–8. This precipitated
the Revolution.

salons: social gatherings, first among the aristocracy, later
among the bourgeoisie, at which ideas were discussed.
They were an important part of the intellectual life of the
eighteenth century, and some of them have become
legendary.

sans-culottes: the politically active small property owners and
superior artisans who provided much of the motive power
of the Terror.

Sections: the 48 units of local government into which Paris was
divided by the municipal law of June 1790.

Septembriseurs: the *sans-culottes* and *fédérés*, etc., who were the
'executioners' at the time of the September Massacres.

sociétés populaires: local clubs, important after 1791, many of
them affiliated to the Jacobin Club in Paris. Since they
tended to advocate extremist views, they were controlled
by the Revolutionary Government of the Terror and many
were suppressed on the fall of Hébert.

suspects: those whose revolutionary orthodoxy was called in
question; not necessarily nobles.

taxation populaire: the compulsory sale, usually conducted by
the *sans-culottes*, of necessary foodstuffs and household
goods, at an arbitrary and low price.

Thermidor: Revolutionary month of July/August; when referred
to by itself generally meaning the crisis when Robespierre
fell (9–10 Thermidor).

terriers: registers of feudal dues. The registers were renewed
from time to time, but in the second half of the eighteenth
century extensive revisions, as part of the 'feudal reaction'
made them the object of peasant hatred and they were
burnt in many places during the *grande peur*.

The Terror: the method of emergency government between
September 1793 and July 1794, when the reserve powers
of the State were used to direct the whole national life. It
is this period that prefigures modern totalitarianism.

vicaire: the assistant to the parish priest (*curé*).

venal offices: those offices in the administration which could be
purchased. They often became hereditary, and the
abolition of 'venality', which meant opening these offices
to talent, was a prime demand of the Third Estate.

Appendix II

OFFICERS OF THE GREAT COMMITTEE OF PUBLIC SAFETY, JULY 1793 – JULY 1794

previously members of the Dantonist Committee
    Bertrand Barère (1755–1841)
    Robert Lindet (1746–1825)
elected 5 June 1793
    Marie-Jean Hérault de Séchelles (1759–94) *Executed 5 April*
    Georges Couthon (1755–94)   *Executed at Thermidor*
    Louis Saint-Just (1767–94)   *Executed at Thermidor*
elected 22 June 1793
    Jeanbon Saint-André (1749–1813)
    Prieur de la Marne (1756–1827)
elected 27 July 1793
    Maximilien Robespierre (1758-94)   *Executed at Thermidor*
elected 14 August 1793
    Lazare Carnot (1753–1823)
    Prieur de la Côte d'Or (1763–1827)
elected 6 September 1793
    Jean-Nicolas Billaud-Varenne (1756–1819)
    Jean-Marie Collot d'Herbois (1750–96)

N.B. I have specifically excluded the aristocratic 'de'. Where 'de' appears it is part of the name at this stage of the Revolution, and does not imply status.

Appendix III

THE REVOLUTIONARY CALENDER[1]

R. Day	Vendémiaire *Sept*	Brumaire *Oct*	Frimaire *Nov*	Nivôse *Dec*	Pluviôse *Jan*	Ventôse *Feb*	Germinal *March*	Floréal *April*	Prairial *May*	Messidor *June*	Thermidor *July*	Fructidor *Aug*
1	22	22	21	21	20	19	21	20	20	19	19	18
2	23	23	22	22	21	20	22	21	21	20	20	19
3	24	24	23	23	22	21	23	22	22	21	21	20
4	25	25	24	24	23	22	24	23	23	22	22	21
5	26	26	25	25	24	23	25	24	24	23	23	22
6	27	27	26	26	25	24	26	25	25	24	24	23
7	28	28	27	27	26	25	27	26	26	25	25	24
8	29	29	28	28	27	26	28	27	27	26	26	25
9	30	30	29	29	28	27	29	28	28	27	27	26
10	*Oct* 1	31	30	30	29	28	30	29	29	28	28	27
11	2	*Nov* 1	*Dec* 1	31	30	*March* 1	31	30	30	29	29	28
12	3	2	2	*Jan* 1	31	2	*April* 1	*May* 1	31	30	30	29
13	4	3	3	2	*Feb* 1	3	2	2	*June* 1	*July* 1	31	30
14	5	4	4	3	2	4	3	3	2	2	*Aug* 1	31
15	6	5	5	4	3	5	4	4	3	3	2	*Sept* 1
16	7	6	6	5	4	6	5	5	4	4	3	2
17	8	7	7	6	5	7	6	6	5	5	4	3
18	9	8	8	7	6	8	7	7	6	6	5	4
19	10	9	9	8	7	9	8	8	7	7	6	5
20	11	10	10	9	8	10	9	9	8	8	7	6
21	12	11	11	10	9	11	10	10	9	9	8	7
22	13	12	12	11	10	12	11	11	10	10	9	8
23	14	13	13	12	11	13	12	12	11	11	10	9
24	15	14	14	13	12	14	13	13	12	12	11	10
25	16	15	15	14	13	15	14	14	13	13	12	11
26	17	16	16	15	14	16	15	15	14	14	13	12
27	18	17	17	16	15	17	16	16	15	15	14	13
28	19	18	18	17	16	18	17	17	16	16	15	14
29	20	19	19	18	17	19	18	18	17	17	16	15
30	21	20	20	19	18	20	19	19	18	18	17	16

Jours sans-culottides

1	17
2	18
3	19
4	20
5	21

[1] The Revolutionary (or Republican) Calendar was in official use between 22 September 1793 (1 Vendémiaire of the Year Two) to the end of 1805 (11 Nivôse of the Year Fourteen). In leap-years (1796, 1800, 1804), 11 Ventôse corresponded to 29 February and the extra day of the Republican Year was 'found' by adding a sixth *jour sans-culottide* (or *jour complémentaire*) to the five shown above.

Index

This index itself provides an interesting comment on the literary tradition of the Revolution as a holocaust. It contains the names of the leading nobles and commoners who were concerned directly with the daily events of the Revolution: allowing for the fact that some nobles (and others) fled as *émigrés*, and that the index cannot pretend to be anything but an indication, for it is not a survey, nevertheless it records simply that more leaders survived than died.

Executed or assassinated		*Survived or died of natural causes*
Nobles	6	23
Commoners	18	19